PRESERVED FOR GREATNESS

Life Changing Strategies for Recovery

Rev. Aaron Jamal Ph.D.

FAITH LEGACIES
PLANTING GOOD WORKS
TO PRODUCE GOOD FRUIT

Table of Contents

AN INTRODUCTION

It was a hot evening. We lived in one of the most densely populated areas on the south side of Chicago. Some called it the "Concrete Jungle." This place we called home was the Robert Taylor Projects. There was a lot of violence, gangs, drugs and the like.

On this evening, a few friends that I normally played with and I were sitting outside discussing sports, music, and whatever small talk that came up, when suddenly, there was a stirring that appeared to be coming towards us. There was a crowd of people shouting and running in our direction. As the noise drew closer, we stopped talking and began paying attention. Soon it became apparent what was causing the stirring.

A local gang, called "The Imperial Pimp Rangers" was drafting people in the neighborhood. Members of the gang approached us and very aggressively began grabbing and pulling on some of my friends. Each one that they pulled up from the benches we sat on was compelled to respond to shouts of: "where you live?", "how old are you?", "Represent! Who you wit?" Frightened and intimidated, all of those sitting next to me were selected and ordered to come to an initiation meeting. Anticipating that I would be selected next, I stood up and waited for the same line of questioning. "Ain't that lil' Mike?" one of them asked. Surprised by the new question, I said nothing. "Your brother named *Mike*?" he asked. "Yeah, that's my brother." I said, confused by the special treatment I was getting.

"You go home... This ain't for you." He said as they walked away leaving me all alone.

I looked around and began wondering why I was not selected. I was not interested in joining a gang but I was confused by the fact that out of all of my friends, I was the only one not drafted. Maybe it was because of my brother Mike, but there appeared to be a screening component that prevented my selection.

This happened often through my childhood. It was as though I was protected by some incredible force. I had a childhood friend that recognized how things usually worked out for me and he said, "Aaron, it's like you in the mafia man. Anybody mess with you is gonna get messed up." I laughed but admitted it did seem rather strange.

Even when it seemed as though trouble had finally caught up with me, I would seldom receive the same consequences as others. For example: While walking in an area of a rival gang, I was spotted as someone that didn't belong there and so they chased me and shot at me. I ran as fast as I could and sprinted across the Dan Ryan expressway in the afternoon. I should have been hit by a bullet from the guns of my aggressors or at least one of the cars or trucks that were speeding down the express lanes. Strangely, I ran across untouched. I heard a bullet ricochet off of the pavement as I ran, but not one of them hit me.

Exhausted from the running and the excitement of being shot at, I rested between two parked cars and hid out of sight. It finally dawned on me that I had just sprinted crossed 6 lanes of traffic without getting hit and I thought... "Wow that was close. God must be looking out for me."

I would live for another 35 years before I finally arrived at this opportunity that I appeared uniquely targeted and equipped to address. I had no idea that I was being preserved for such a time as this. After a number of "once in a lifetime" types of experiences, I stood in front of a uniquely challenged people that God would knit to me and our staff as we discovered what it really meant to be "Preserved for Greatness."

Rev. Dr. Martin Luther King Jr. declared he had a dream of an entirely different world than the one he was living in and challenged the present world to change. He did not adjust his dream to adapt to the current circumstances, but rather bucked against odds that appeared insurmountable.

The vision and boldness that drove our Preserved for Greatness program targeted a people that were stigmatized and oppressed through years of failed models by both secular and faith communities. Our target population consisted of people screaming for a set of principles key to unlocking their hopes and redeeming their value as men and women of destiny. These people may have been misfits, but they were not mistakes or waste to be discarded. These people were, more than not, certain of their impotence to change their circumstances through their own power.

We introduced them to a hope and dream that promised greatness rather than diminished obscurity. We introduced principles of empathy and social interdependence that helped them to experience belonging where they were once isolated and rejected.

This story outgrew initial plans to harness the collective intellect of a few leaders in order to run a pilot program. Innovation challenged faith, and community organizations to work with state and federal agencies to serve the same client in order to reach optimum results.

We challenged the skeptics that doubted our abilities to move aside for a dream. Our dream was not too hard for our God. Our dream would knit us together as interchangeable servers and leaders determined to achieve greatness.

Although the journey of this program spanned a few years, the life changing principles have survived and live today. I give thanks to all that sacrificed and dedicated their lives toward the manifestation of that dream.

In a room crowded with men and women from the south side, west side, and suburbs of Chicago stood a rather tall Black man I will call Miller. Miller was sharply dressed. His outerwear was meticulously put together as one that was accustomed to presenting himself as "in charge." Miller did nothing to hide the scowl on his face that projected his skepticism about yet another "program." He walked in and around the room and sat down among the rest of his peers. They arrived together but appeared completely independent in their personal expectations for what we had to offer. This was the first official meeting of our newly revised ATR substance abuse recovery program.

There was a steady volume of mumbling in the atmosphere that seemed to quiet as I entered the room. I walked toward the table that had a wireless microphone on it and picked it up in order to make certain that I would be heard without shouting. I prepared a greeting in my mind, being careful not to ask them "how you doing?" because I knew that many of them did not want to be there. Most of the people had not slept in their own homes or apartments and most had been directed here as a choice between a sentence pointing them toward jail or a program that was supposed to help them.

Irritated from having to sit too close to one another, social clicks began to formulate their own seating arrangements. Miller, however, appeared to be examining me as he looked me over and asked what others wanted to know. "You da man?" he asked. I smiled and gave him a confirming nod but waited for the volume to calm just a bit more before I spoke. Miller stood up and shouted at his peers "The man is ready talk to us if you can bring it down just a bit!" I thanked him and made a mental note that he was comfortable taking charge of a room without invitation.

Using the microphone that had already been tested for volume I spoke; "Good morning!" I paused for a response and with some hesitation a few responded with "good morning." I handed the microphone to one of the other staff members and he began introducing me as the CEO and Director of the facility and then said "I'm gonna get out of his way, cause he's gonna tell you what's up!" He handed me the microphone and this time there was less grumbling and so I spoke.

Miller tilted his head toward the side, as though he were slightly annoyed and asked, "You got a name?" "Most call me Pastor Jamal." I replied into the microphone so all could hear the exchange. I proceeded to lay out a few ground rules that were unique to our facility with an emphasis on several signs printed in color that were posted on the wall and read "NO Profanity!" I gave no explanation for the signs but stated that there would only be two warnings concerning that rule before being asked to leave the room if there was a third offense.

I was certain that this population was very familiar with rules even if they appeared compelled to break them. Another certainty was that they were a group that held a common disdain for people that appeared to look down on them. This was a captive audience, but not very enthused about "another program." I nodded to one of my co-workers and he lowered the lighting so I could begin the presentation. I directed several people to rearrange their seating so they could make room for the presentation to be projected onto the wall. I was careful to test the sound system's volume. I wanted this first impression of our program to grab them, and it did.

Armed with a PowerPoint presentation embedded with sound, video clips and graphics, I introduced them to something that clearly caught their attention. There was an assortment of video clips borrowed from the movie, "The Matrix." The selected scene of lead character "Morpheus" explaining to "Neo" about the truth that he was blinded from, prompted them to lean forward in their seats. Morpheus stated that Neo was a slave, born into a prison that he could not smell, taste or touch... a prison for his mind. Every eye appeared focused on the presentation.

In a follow up clip, Morpheus tells Neo about a system that is their enemy that exists all around them. He tells of how this system held people from all walks of life. He also said many of them were so hopelessly dependent on the system and were not ready to be unplugged. He further explained that some of them would even fight to protect this system. This very popular and powerful drama and illustration seemed to open the minds of our new guests and strike a chord of acceptance. We wanted to introduce our members to a new world of possibilities, a new level of expectations, a new "Matrix."

We have since learned that many people rarely exceed their greatest expectations of life. If they stop believing that they are *more* than the stigmas that haunt them because of their diseased past, then they will *never* pursue the improbable dreams of their youth.

Rather than the failed, shameful low expectations that framed the discarded and despairing reality many were trying to escape, Preserved for Greatness (affectionately called *P4G*) provided a priceless hope for a new and amazing future. P4G framed those extraordinary expectations in the hearts and minds of those within our group. We hoped to share a glimpse of the life changing principles we learned in order to set these captives free from addiction.

I drew their attention to the name of our program "Preserved for Greatness" and explained why we posted that phrase. I assured the group that beyond the triggers, thoughts, urges and relapses was an achievable life that was free and sober. I also pointed out that we were aware that some were probably in the midst of a cycle that was similar to that "song that never ends" and were probably considering getting high even while I was talking.

I panned the room, holding the microphone in hand and noticed some of the members were sitting back in their seats looking as though they would be nodding any minute. "But now" I shouted! "Now is an opportunity to prove to the critics and yourselves that they were wrong" I continued shouting to them. Surprised by the sudden burst of volume and passion, some began to nervously stir as I began to walk the room. "You have been preserved for greatness and greatness never comes from doing the same things you've always done! Greatness comes from innovation and the greatest innovators in the world have come from circumstances that are just as difficult as yours" I said.

I paused, panning the room to see if I still had their attention and continued. "If you want what you've never had, you must be willing to do what you've never done! I know that some of you are experts on the system. But let us introduce you to a truth that's held you captive as a slave and another truth that can set you free! Now is there anyone here that wants to be set free?" I shouted and indicated that I wanted them to raise their hands if they wanted to be set free. Some raised their hands but not all.

"Freedom does not happen accidentally! It must be taken by force! You won't have to do this alone but you will have to be an active participant! Now stand on your feet if you are ready to be set free!" I shouted and then waited to see the level of commitment. With some level of hesitancy, each of them began to stand.

Rev. Dr. Martin Luther King Jr. said *"The ultimate measure of a man is not where he stands* **in moments of comfort**, *but where he stands* **at times of challenge and controversy.**" I told this group that the truth we had for them was not to make them comfortable while they wasted away, but was intended to prepare them to stand in the midst of challenges that will come.

As I panned the room I saw faces that appeared to have a glimmer of hope. Maybe we understood what they were struggling with. Maybe this was not just *"another program."* However, the truth they sought was deeper than just their existence as slaves. We needed to take off the blind folds of addiction and show them that there was an alternative to the addiction that had enslaved them. We needed to awaken them to dreams once filled with the boisterous audacity of hope that had grown silent.

We needed to gain more than the *interest* of our members. We needed to gain their *trust*. Gaining their trust is very difficult when many have been carrying the reputations of being a failure, liar, loser, thief, untrustworthy and a loss cause. People that do not consider themselves trustworthy are rarely trusting. Therefore, gaining their trust would also require strategies to make them more trustworthy.

Gaining their trust was oddly more difficult for us *because* we were a faith-based program. We were very much aware of the stigmatizations that followed faith-based organizations as well. In some cases, we had to overcome disappointments associated with our members' childhood experiences with the church. At the same time, the members had to overcome recent experiences of shallow, religious traditions that at best exchanged one compulsive behavior for another. Some had been indoctrinated to believe that "preachers" knew nothing about what it was like to overcome addiction and that this program was only a political ploy to gain faith-based votes. Some members had never really been to church or spoken with a pastor before. They had only seen them in the neighborhood, on television or heard them on the radio.

Gaining their trust to specifically address addiction was multifaceted. We needed to develop *new* thinking patterns while developing *new* responses to life's trials as *new* habits. The new habits would re-shape their character in order to remap their destiny. Our strategies were consistent with the old maxim: "*Sow a thought, reap an action; sow an action, reap a habit; sow a habit, reap a character; sow a character, reap a destiny.*"

For the purpose of illuminating the basis of our approach toward habits, I will use Stephen Covey's definition of a habit: "[1]the intersection of knowledge, skills, and desire." All three were required in order to form the new habits.

Forming the new habit also required an effective plan to facilitate the desire. To implement the plan we applied lessons learned from observing the Apollo astronauts as they broke free from the earth's gravitational pull. There was more energy used during the lift off and the earliest few miles than was used over the next several days to travel over ½ of a million miles. Likewise, our plan was to establish as many liberating encounters consecutively as possible in order to introduce and develop lasting new skills and new habits.

Our program schedules were based on all day sessions initially, rather than weekly encounters because sustainable habits were impossible to develop with such infrequent occurrences.

Habits, good or bad, have their own gravitational pull. If members were to break free from bad habits then we

---

[1] "Seven Habits of Highly Effective People" pg 22 , Published by Franklin Covey 1990

would need more than the under-estimates of 21-28 days to accomplish that. One may learn to perform an act within a brief time, but new habits are far more difficult to establish.

Additionally, the disease component of addiction is consistent with [2]"a disorder in humans,...with recognizable signs and often having a known cause." The causal affects of this disease are not as variable as the methodologies used to address the disorder. Clearly this is not something that you can just take a pill, or shot to conquer. Our members did not respond to pharmaceutical remedies alone. Impaired cognitive skills contributed to behavioral patterns that demonstrated socially, mentally, and physically destructive compulsive habits.

The "*different situations*" that they expressed as root causes for their addictions was consistent with the majority of our members. However, the *consistent* element of our most effective plan remains the "*caring people*" who implement the plan. I don't know of anyone that has broken free from this disorder without the assistance of *someone*. We are at least as valuable as the principles that are guiding us. *Everyone* was required to establish this *greatness*.

We had people from all walks of life. We had teachers, managers, sales people, mothers, fathers, teens, adults, veterans, gang members, prostitutes and career

---

[2] Encarta Dictionary "Disease"

criminals, just to name a few. Our members required principles that possessed universal application. And we were determined to deliver them with empathy and clarity.

Our stated goal to the members was to help them realize the "Greatness" they were preserved to become and demonstrate. We strived to maximize our efforts to impart knowledge, develop skills and reshape desires. Greatness like excellence must be established as a habit. The Greek philosopher Aristotle states the following: *"We are what we repeatedly do. Excellence, then, is not an act, but a habit."*

We tried to introduce and establish principles that each of our members would be able to adopt. Stephen Covey wrote: [3]*"... principles are deep, fundamental truths that have universal application. ... When these truths are internalized into habits, they empower people to create a wide variety of practices to deal with different situations."*

Ironically, the challenge of gaining trust from this resistant group while presenting universal principles was somehow ideal for my history and set of skills. Raised on the south side of Chicago, in a family of 11 siblings, I had no problem empathizing with the hard luck stories many of them wore as a badge of honor. Most of our staff was raised in difficult settings and yet,

---

[3] Seven Habits of Highly Effective People pg 16 IBID

we were all convinced that we had been "Preserved for Greatness!"

MY STORY

I had heard the rehearsed stories of rejection and failed attempts at gaining employment or succeeding in relationships. But we had our own stories of survival as well. "I haven't always been a pastor ya know" I told a large group of participants. I shared my own experiences growing up in the *Robert Taylor Projects* and dealing with violence and drug related battles.

My older brother and sister were both instrumental in introducing me to drugs. Just as with the others that I was fortunate enough to serve in this program, I became exposed to the degrading effects of drugs on my social and moral barometer. Allow me to briefly introduce you to the origins of my influences - both good and bad.

My earliest childhood memories had distinctive boundaries of right and wrong that protected me from much of the risk factors rooted within my culture. Even though I was afforded an education in Catholic schools, and attended church on most Sundays, I was living in Robert Taylor Projects. Therefore, I witnessed a lot of violence that was traumatic. I was also shot at before the age of 10 and that was traumatic as well. Additionally, I was drawn to the sensual lures of the shapely young girls in my class rooms and found myself fantasizing about what it would be like to get past 2nd base with more than one of them. That also proved to be a worthy trial for a teen hoping to avoid teen-pregnancy.

However, as the youngest boy in a family of 12 children, I had a lot of eyes on me that were protective and preventive. Without placing judgment on my mother and father's contributions to my upbringing, I believe that my brothers and sisters were in many ways my protection and my guidance through most of my childhood.

My admiration of the athletic skills of one of my older brother's led me to sports. He was what we called "*a baller.*" He was so good in whatever sport he played, I got picked just because I was his brother. The disciplines and perseverance I developed in sports provided a lot of the focus and decision making skills needed to keep me on track and out of trouble. I owe that to my coach. I would need all of those skills to fulfill the dreams I had as a child.

Among the strongest influences of my childhood was music. The variant of influences that I experienced through the LPs and 45s I heard my siblings playing developed a hunger to hear and play music. In addition to a wide selection of records, my Aunt and Uncle, who were famous as legendary Jazz and Blues artists, became pivotal in framing my dreams.

I was fascinated once I realized that my mother's sister, *Abbey Lincoln*, was also this amazing singer /composer /actress that astonished everyone that heard her. I was also infatuated with the fact that her husband, Max Roach, was among the most talented drummers in the world. "These were my relatives? Are you kidding me? But I'm just a big head boy living in the projects. How did I wind up in *their* family?" Those were just a few of the questions I had going through my head. However, I would often dream and daydream about one day reaching fame and fortune in the music industry as well.

But before I could even write my first melody or tap out my first beat, my mother expressed that she was extremely uncomfortable with me "hanging out" with my Uncle Max. I had no exposure to what he was doing privately, but I overheard my mother saying that Uncle Max had a problem with heroin. I didn't care about that and just wanted to follow in his steps as a musician. I had no attraction to drugs or alcohol, but I really wanted to play like he played. Maybe some of that awesome talent would rub off on me.

I was determined to play and my mother was just going to have to understand... right? Well, if you could have met my mother back in the 60s, maybe then you would understand why I had to redirect my interests *away* from playing like Uncle Max. When my mother said "no", she meant "no", and I knew better than to challenge her about this. In those days, that could be dangerous to my health.

Nevertheless, we did have a piano in our home for most of my childhood, courtesy of my oldest sister, and I learned to play it almost out of frustration. I wanted to play something and if this was all that I had, then I would use it. My Aunt and Uncle were pleased to find out that I was playing but neither was close enough to me to offer the personal guidance to prepare me for the lures of drugs and sex associated with that life style. In due time, I was fortunate to travel and perform on national and international tours and to record with a long list of major recording artists. Ultimately, I signed a major recording contract with Atlantic records as a keyboardist/vocalist/composer with "Amuzement Park Band."

Each of my musical opportunities served my goals in fulfilling my musical dreams and provided me with favor to excel. However, I knew I would never have lived long enough to experience that level of success if not for the protection and influence of my siblings. My brothers and sisters were quite proud of my musical accomplishments.

THIS TIME IT'S PERSONAL

It was about 3:30 AM as I was driving down the Dan Ryan Expressway heading to my south side apartment. I had just finished playing a gig on the north side of Chicago. I played in a hot Jazz / Fusion group that was playing to a very faithful following. I was still feeling really good about the show, when out of the corner of my eye, I saw headlights coming toward me.

I was in the left lane with *nowhere* to turn *away* from the impact of the oncoming vehicle. Even before I had a chance to hit the brakes, the oncoming car was driving me into the guard railing and wall. They separated the Expressway from the EL tracks that divided the southbound and northbound expressways.

I don't remember an audible voice, but I distinctly remember hearing "duck", and during a trauma that appeared to be unfolding in slow motion, I ducked. Having ducked, my car hit the guard rail going at least 55 mph because I had no time to hit the brakes.

My face was propelled into the dashboard where the contact crushed my nose and lanced my face underneath my eyes. I was a bloody mess. There was a towel on the seat that I had used previously to dry the sweat that was still pouring off of me from the heat of the club. I pulled the towel toward me and it quickly turned red with blood. It didn't take me long to realize that this blood was *flowing* from my face and that meant I was badly hurt.

Dazed and stunned by the impact, I looked upward toward the passenger window and saw someone that looked like a police officer. "Can you walk?" he asked me. Confused about what had happened, I nodded my head and said "no." "I'm gonna get you an ambulance... you hold on ok?" he shouted to me. I tried to clear my head and asked "what happened?" "You got hit by a drunk driver... helps on the way" he said just before he disappeared.

My bruises must have been pretty bad because the plastic surgeon that restored my nose needed to see my license to get an idea of what I looked like *before* the accident. "I'm going to fix you up like new" the doctor said reassuring me that I would be ok.

It took more than 52 stitches to my face and reconstructive surgery to my crushed nose to put me back together again. My car was completely totaled. When I finally saw the damage to the car, I saw that there were just a few inches between the steering wheel and the back of the driver's seat. The disturbing revelation of my near fatality troubled me to the point of tears.

If I had not ducked, I would have been crushed between the seat and steering wheel or worse. Regrettably, I was not wearing a seat belt. I could have been thrown out through the front windshield.

Tragically, I was one of many people who had been struck by a drunk driver that weekend. I never met the driver, but heard later that the D.A. would be bringing charges. I am sure there was a story behind this man being so out of control that he had to get drunk before ramming his car into me. However, this event formed a story for me as well.

The memories tied to this drunk driver story served to shape the urgency I have about helping people that are in self-destruct mode and struggling with alcoholism or substance abuse. I became determined that we must help them before they hurt themselves and us.

Unfortunately, I learned that one of my older brothers and one of my older sisters were deeply entrenched with addiction as well. It was as though my older brother followed the heroin path of my Uncle Max. I never even knew he was using it. I discovered that my brother had a problem after I graduated and was already touring. Later, I found out that my older sister also had a drug problem. Neither one had previously expressed their using drugs was a problem. They said they were doing just fine. Nevertheless, my brother was the first to ultimately admit he was trapped and needed help.

My modest levels of fame had no ability to help them deal with their addictions. They had been quite instrumental in protecting me from a lot of the risk factors surrounding my childhood, but I appeared impotent in being able to help *them* to deal with *their* addictions.

I tried to use my gift to help my brother by coming to perform at a recovery house where he resided. My wife and I appeared and sang and played songs that touched their hearts. For at least that night, I made my brother proud.

But those experiences failed to give me the insights I needed to help my older brother and sister. Those experiences made for interesting conversation and even inspired some lyrics to some of the songs I wrote. Regrettably, they did nothing to remedy the struggles of my older brother and sister.

After I lost my brother and then my sister to addiction related illnesses, my passion to address compulsive behaviors, and addiction specifically, was catapulted into a lifelong search for effective strategies. I was particularly troubled by the loss of my brother because I was instrumental in leading him to Christ and participated in his baptism. I mistakenly believed his battle with drugs was over.

However, when it came to sustained sobriety, I was clueless in providing the stabilizing structure needed. I became familiar with 12-step programs that taught about drug avoidance, 7-step models and Christian versions of the same. I found more agreement with Christian versions of the 12 step models. On the other hand, I was still not convinced that these were comprehensively addressing the sudden and unexpected changes during this recovery from chemical dependencies, compulsive behaviors, and the like.

I faced a dilemma with a combination of privilege and lack, and I was not managing either well. I had an enjoyable level of popularity and accomplishment.

However, I was clearly lacking self-control and empathy for others. I was blessed with a family of my own - with children and a beautiful wife. Still, I lacked the sacrificial love that would put them above my own selfish quests.

I was *blessed* with creative abilities to write and arrange songs that appeared marketable enough for other musicians, singers and producers to lend me their talents toward a recording contract or live performance. However, I also *lacked* the perseverance needed to stay the course so that all could benefit from that potential. All of my blessings were far more than I deserved and I knew that unless I got help I would blow it all.

There was no excuse for my behaving irresponsibly, lying, or engaging in lewd and sexually immoral behavior. "Dealing with me" was among the hardest challenges I had ever faced. I became far more empathic about some of the compulsive disorders I shared in common with my siblings.

Why was I doing the very things I didn't want to do and not doing the things I loved? I was out of control! After trying synthetic solutions such as drugs and alcohol, things progressively got worse. I was even *more* out of control.

I had exposure to drugs and indulged in a lifestyle that could have easily contributed to an untimely death. But I was spared. My escape was not because of my own skills or modest levels of fame or any other admirable qualities. The mercy of God almighty alone kept me from the consequences of my own destructive behaviors.

To make a much longer story shorter, I benefitted from the prayers and intercession of a loving Mother-in-law. She prayed and loved me unconditionally. I don't know what the content of her prayers were, but I witnessed the outcome. God moved in my life as only God could. He protected me from behaviors and consequences that could have easily led to prison or death. He revealed His Love to me and I drew closer to Him. I'm not talking about *religion*. I'm talking about a *relationship* that is intimate and without any pretense. I cried on more than a few occasions about being frustrated and lost and He heard my cry.

Due to the mercy, grace and supernatural power of God Almighty, I am set free! That's right, I am free! No, I did not go through a 12 step or a 7 step program but I am free and sober! I have heard of others that say they were truly helped by 12 step modeled programs, and I am happy for them. This is not an indictment against any effective 12 step program. I am just sharing that in this, and in many other cases, God alone gets the glory.

Now I am profoundly aware that my testimony is not the same testimony for everyone that has come to establish a relationship with the Lord. I also recognize that just as I was preserved from many of the risk factors of my childhood, I was also preserved from many of the disorders associated with addiction. Again, I don't claim any credit for the interventions and blessings that preserved me, and I am most certain that it was not happenstance that I was preserved.

In my case and many others, the intervention that happened for me came through the relationships I had with people. People are among the most effective tools in aiding someone who is serious about recovering from a compulsive disorder. It is my belief that God's healing power is leveraged through people. Therefore I don't see my faith challenged by those that would claim they had a part in my healing or recovery. God uses people to do His will. That is what He has done throughout history and He is still doing it today. God Almighty has a plan for many and I am fortunate to be part of that plan. I am also *humbled* that He is revealing that plan to me and others day by day. I am still in the developmental stages for the greatness that I believed I was preserved for, and I am forever grateful that God is not through with me yet.

THE DRIVING FORCE

Like too many other people in this nation, I lost both of my siblings to addictive related illnesses. After their untimely deaths, I mourned and experienced a brief era of frustration.

Previously, I had been allowed to pray for others and watched the manifestation of their healings and deliverance. I even watched in awe of the power of God casting out spirits right in front of me. Why wouldn't that same God use me to help my brother and sister? I couldn't figure it out. My faith in God was not challenged, but I was less confident in my own competencies.

I was still compelled to help people associated with this disease and continued to pray and seek education, opportunity and wisdom. I was never one to sit back and do nothing, but I had no real venue or opportunity to make a difference. My wife, a gift from heaven, saw my frustration and passion as well. God used her to help me to plan and facilitate my vision to help people with addiction disorders.

Finally, I could shake off the frustration and recognize that *Preserved for Greatness* presented an opportunity to do something extraordinary. We were not going to stand by and watch people die. This was not a time for tradition. This was a time for extraordinary measures. At such a time as this, we had an opportunity to break destructive cycles of compulsion. We were uniquely positioned to hold up a light in a very dark room and illuminate a way out. We had an opportunity to develop greatness in others.

THE "SNACKER" DAYS

That greatness would not come without sacrifice and we certainly sacrificed a lot at first. In retrospect, I can laugh at all of the incredible things we did in hopes of really launching this program. But make no mistake about it; this was very hard to pull off.

I was fortunate enough to have a wife that was at least as optimistic as I was about the potential of this program. I could see the potential and I could see that we were qualified, but the maze and journey we went through to actually get paid... that was not funny. We were an attractive collaborative and earned the favor and respect of the Director of D.A.S.A. She was a strong leader and was open for innovation. Without her leadership, I doubt that Illinois would have lifted this program off the floor.

There were several false starts and unforeseen challenges that plagued the first 6 months of the launched Access to Recovery (ATR) program. We had an overhead that was large and we could barely afford to buy two $.99 "Snackers" from KFC for our lunch. The manager of the KFC across the street was so impressed with our dedication that she would sometimes throw an extra sandwich in the bag for encouragement. We humbly and graciously accepted and thanked her. Affectionately, we called this period our "Snacker Days."

We were still diligently making plans for a flood of participants that we anticipated coming to our facility. As it would happen, the first person that enrolled in our program, came as an accident. He was sent to *another* location that was not even setup for intake. They referred him to our location and we got our first *member*.

He must have wondered what was going on because he got sooooo much attention. We were all tripping over each other trying to serve him because we were all desperate for an opportunity to show how good we could be. It must have impressed him because he came back and continued with the program. He eventually admitted it was kind of weird being the only member in the program but we let him feel "special" and continued to give him the best of what we had to offer. We even shared our "Snackers" which were valuable commodities whenever we came out of our classes.

Dr. Margaret was a gifted Program Director and the program design she put together had depth and a very high quality of customer service built in. We spent a lot of time trying to encourage one another about things getting better and continued to train regarding the use of the presentations that we had designed for the membership. Our administrative staff must have thought I was out of my mind because I kept holding workshops on handling volume calls and a high volume of members. We would "brain storm" (*and dream*) every day on the promise of having a great deal of members coming to what they believed was the best substance abuse recovery program in the state.

We visited other sites to see what they were doing and how things had progressed for them. It seemed as though everyone was waiting for this ATR program to *really* launch.

We continued to build relationships and Linkage Agreements with as many people and organizations as we could. We sold our program as the best kept secret in town. However, we knew that if it remained a secret it would die even before it was launched. Because this was voucher driven, we relied on referrals for all of our traffic.

Frustrated with the slow pace of referrals, we decided that we had to get aggressive or die. We pleaded with state leadership to allow us to market our program to potential candidates and have them screened and enrolled at or near our facility. It was a gutsy request and DASA (*Dept. of Alcoholism and Substance Abuse*) was accommodating because the program was still in the infant stages and they recognized the need for innovation.

We designed flyers that were culturally appropriate and eye appealing to our target population. It cost us another investment, but paid off in a big way. The flyers served to help brand our name and opened the door to even more linkage agreements with other housing providers. The membership that came to the program was pleased with what we were giving them, but there were a variety of unforeseen challenges that we needed to address as we grew.

Dr. Margaret was also able to design an awesome database that allowed us to track our membership activities. We were able to enter contact information that populated data with the services that were assessed for each member, and then schedule the classes for each day, for each provider and for each member. It was genius. We knew that at some point there would be a time of accounting for the activities and services we were billing for and we were able to provide computer generated reports internally and quickly.

Each of us was using whatever talents we had to increase the efficiency of our program. Pastor Brady was known for his boldness and charm to meet and greet. You could hear him talking from down the street even if your windows were closed. He had a contagious laugh that disarmed even the skeptics. Therefore he was drafted to be the head of the outreaching effort for our program.

Pastor Dave was a one man, one car, *Transportation Company* that helped us to overcome some of the problems that members faced getting to the facility during the early stages of the program. It was hard work but it was exciting! People were experiencing life changing classes and we loved it!

We owed a lot of the success we were experiencing to the many people that agreed to assist us. We learned about how to fill out the required paper work from DASA's staff as well as the policies and procedures that helped our site to be approved. We also got assistance from DASA as did other providers to learn the online interface required for reporting. That was a great relief because we were spending 8-12 hours just to prepare the reports needed to initiate our payments. Then we delivered them to downtown Chicago where we had to pay for parking and then wait while they were scrutinized. This was always tense because we depended on their approval in order to get paid. These reports were required to be neatly organized and mistakes could prove very costly because until they were reconciled payment was delayed.

All of this occurred weeks after we had already served members and spent dollars on everything from rent to phone, to lights, to gas just to keep the doors open. I hope you can feel some of the anxiety we all experienced during those initial days. Every ATR organization had red tape stories.

Those days proved to shape our character and prove how serious we were about doing this program. Giving all credit due to the members, some were very patient with us because they could tell that the program was still developing and were flexible as we continued to evolve.

We had thrown 100% of our efforts, finances, and resources toward making this work. Quitting was not an option! In a way, we needed this to work as much as the membership did. After the first year of the program, we began to establish our name and impact across the city.

The greatest asset we held to excel in this program was that we felt genuine love for these members. We felt no judgment for their faults because their faults were no greater than our own. We made no attempts to proselytize them. Our tools of indoctrinating and transformation were summed up in the way we loved them, served them and educated them.

I had been mentored by the late Rev. Hazel Fort. Rev. Fort held a number of titles, however, the privileged few that saw her with any level of frequency called her "Mother" or "Rev." Some even called her "Reverend Mother" just to make sure she got her proper respect. In a neighborhood overflowing with violence, poverty, addiction, broken families and death, Mother was as a beacon of light. This woman had the boldness to confront evil and the love to embrace the rejected. Her genuine love gained a reputation and favor with some of the hardest criminals that lived in one of the most dangerous communities in Chicago.

I witnessed more than one request from Mayor Dailey to come and pray for him and the city because he believed she could get a prayer through to God. She was also admired by a few other well known politicians such as Congressman Danny Davis, Alderman Smith as well as Senator Rickey Hendon and former Deputy Superintendent Dana Starks.

Walking along side of Rev. Fort through this crime infested neighborhood taught me that there were no silver bullets to solve the problems of these lives. I learned from her as we traveled through some of the most dangerous streets of Chicago. Mother would say "I may not be able to change their life, that's a job for Jesus! But I can love them. That's the most powerful thing I can do for them, besides prayer, is to love them!"

Rev. Fort's model of service was a bench mark for all of our staff that served within our program. This was the same model that I witnessed personally interceding for me when I was as lost and as confused as these appeared to be in this room. Rev. Fort had an incredible way of making everyone feel as though we were her favorite. I sensed that most of our members had not felt like anyone's favorite for a long time. That became one of our goals.

R.A.T.E.S – FRAMING OUR COLLABORATION

"How to implement five primary principles needed to run an effective organization" was our first task. In a ground level office and conference room were forty to fifty Faith-based leaders. Author and founder of R.A.T.E.S. Foundation a National Heritage Foundation and federal grant reviewer, Rev. Dr. Margaret Jamal, introduced videos and PowerPoint presentations and all were timely and empowering.

R.A.T.E.S. is an acronym for Response-ability, Account-ability, Technical-ability, Evaluation-ability, and Sustain-ability. Under the direction of Rev. Dr. Margaret Jamal we all learned to assess our strengths and challenges as they related to our ability to respond to the needs of our clients, staff, partners and our donors. Additionally we learned how to develop budgets, and reports at a level of efficiency that would be compliant with government standards. As we successfully completed this training we became acutely aware of the need to collaborate with like minded partners. Each of our partners was R.A.T.E.S. Certified and competent in a variety of areas.

The faith community was notorious for not addressing socially relevant issues prevalent in urban areas. I didn't know of one congregation that did not have at least one member or relative struggling with substance abuse. This was an unprecedented opportunity for us to come together and use our synergistic skills and resources to address a devastating disease plaguing our communities.

The lessons we learned in the R.AT.E.S. Certification classes revealed the pain, suffering, or crisis we survived and were most qualified to address. In these classes we discovered how our past trials had uniquely prepared us to acquire the perseverance and character needed to fulfill our most intimate hopes.

There were overlapping skill sets as well as some unique skills that contributed to making us uniquely valuable to each other. Beyond building the competencies for our collaborative was the challenge to frame an interdependent model of independent leaders. We sought a "win-win" philosophy. [4]Stephen Covey wrote: *"Win-win is a frame of mind and heart that constantly seeks mutual benefit in all human interactions. Win-win means that agreements or solutions are mutually beneficial, mutually satisfying."*

Dr. Margaret generously shared a number of funding opportunities that would be coming up soon. Among the list of opportunities was a State funded program called Access to Recovery (ATR). As a result of the Faith Based Initiative signed in to law by President George W. Bush, there were concerted efforts to formulate partnerships that linked faith-based and community social service providers with state and local agencies in order to maximize resources, service, and impact.

---

[4] Seven Habits of Highly Effective People;Pg 103; Stephen Covey. IBID

ATR was a voucher driven program that allowed the clientele to choose where they wanted to receive services. For the first time, one person could choose to receive services from multiple social providers of their choice, funded by federal dollars. This program was being run under the Center for Substance Abuse and Treatment.

Framing the collaborative was the key to our ability to provide an attractive array of services and to reduce our over head. We worked on a compensation plan that provided incentives for partners while covering staffing as well as program related expenditures. The level of budgetary transparency regarding the earning potentials built a level of trust between the partners that resulted in a perception of mutual satisfaction.

Illinois Clergy Association, Brady has a Bunch Ministries, and Apostle C.D. Bush Foundation shared one facility in order to share resources, centralize our intake, and to brand one location. The strategy was unprecedented and challenged current systems to re-think effective models.

We formed mutual agreements of understanding with Housing and Treatment service providers as well as the judicial system that afforded us opportunities to serve a wide range of clientele.

It was imperative that we presented a structured recovery plan. However, that recovery had to be perceived as an achievable goal. Far too many people look at addicts as though they have a terminal disease such as AIDS. Conversely, if there is any chance of surviving AIDS, you need a variety of treatments and supplements that will help build your immune system to identify and fight off infections.

Similarly with addiction, there is a weakened ability to fight off urges which produce cravings to re-engage in to destructive behaviors. However, addiction need not be a life sentence. Millions of people are living sober lives after engaging in addictive behaviors. Some may view that as an overly simplified way of describing a very complex disease. Nevertheless, that was our core premise in initiating our "Circle of Services" that framed the support systems at our facility. Our program required us to reach some short term program goals with long term potential.

We provided a Circle of Services model that surrounded each member with an array of services: Family Counseling, Vocational Training, Life Skills Training, Group Counseling, Peer Coaching, Recovery Coaching, Employment Training, Employment Placement, Individual Counseling, Pastoral Counseling, G.E.D., and Transportation. These services proved to be instrumental in providing a measurably effective impact in the lives of those that sustained beyond a 30 day period of the program.

SHAPING OUR CULTURE

A young man sits in a chair across from a woman that asked him the question: "Why are you here?" The man struggles to make eye contact with the woman that was more interested in filling out the paper work in front of her. He began to share his dilemma with her: "I can't go on like this. If I don't get some help today, I don't know what I will do." Without even looking up at the young man she asks in a very cynical voice: "What's wrong with you?" Careful not to say he felt suicidal because he did not want to be institutionalized, the man said "I sort of thought you could help me figure that out… you know what I'm saying." "What are your symptoms?" the woman said still staring at the paper. "I…I, I don't really know." The man said still struggling to make eye contact with the woman. "Take a seat and someone will call your name", the woman declared motioning toward a waiting area before continuing. "Next!" she shouted as though the man had already left her cubicle.

This man had just experienced what Martin Buber calls an "I-It" encounter. Buber writes:[5] *"When a subject is analyzed as an object, the subject is no longer a Thou, but*

---

[5] [1]Martin Buber, *I and Thou*, translated by Ronald Gregor Smith (New York: Charles Scribner's Sons, 1958), p. 26.

*becomes an **It**. The being which is analyzed as an object is the **It** in an I-It relation.*" The cold and distant "I-It" approach appears typical within the social service community; particularly among communities of color. The caring approaches associated with "I-Thou" relationships require an investment of empathy that is rarely demonstrated by that style of social service providers.

We intentionally framed our facility to adopt what Buber referred to as an "I-Thou" style. [6]*"**I-Thou** is not a means to some object or goal, but is an ultimate relation involving the whole being of each subject"* writes Buber. We resisted calling our program participants "clients" and called them *members*.

Another goal was to build an attitude of inclusion rather than an atmosphere of "us vs. them." We set up a culture of structure and rules that was designed to make our place a "safe haven" for them.

There was a qualifying program selection criterion. Each of the participants confirmed that they had experienced some level of involvement with alcohol and/or drugs that resulted in an encounter with law enforcement. There were various degrees of their involvement with the drug of choice, but each had a

---

[6] [1]Martin Buber, *I and Thou*, translated by Ronald Gregor Smith IBID

story that interconnected with something they used to numb the trauma and quiet the noise of their lives.

Some had co-occurring disorders that were birthed from lives that were more like nightmares from which they seemed to never wake. Others had conflicting existences where they were once "successful" but somehow got so derailed from their path that they forfeited money, relationships and careers. Others were so young when they first began their compulsive behavior that they never advanced toward a career, finished high school, or sustained a long-term relationship. Some were in a perpetual hustle, selling everything from their cars to their children. Equally tragic, were the many cases of the women who bartered their bodies as an item for consumption to continue using their drug of choice.

BEING TRANSFORMED BY RENEWING OUR MINDS

Transformed lives required renewed minds. Our first goals were to address the thought patterns that were toxic to sober life styles. Discipline is a necessary component for establishing new life paths. If you lack discipline you are also lacking the character needed to complete your course. Rather than implementing "steps" that resembled failed strategies, we introduced a customized daily plan that worked on multiple areas of their deficiencies simultaneously. Rather than trying to fit everyone in to a 12-step program, we assessed each members needs and applied a list of services from our circle of services to those needs.

We were not a weekly program, but a *daily* program. We knew that especially in the early stages, our member base required multiple visits per week at a minimum and some as frequently as 5 days per week. To indoctrinate this populous into a new and healthy mindset, we needed to offset years of "stinking thinking." We maximized each visit with a volume of services to engage them over a six to seven hour daily program schedule.

The member I previously introduced as Miller had an extensive history of being incarcerated from the time he was a youth and for most of his adult life. His profile of criminal activity was rather intimidating for our in-take specialist. The specialist quickly brought me Miller's folder and recommended that I attend to this member personally. I accepted the recommendation and arranged a meeting later that afternoon.

Sitting across the table from Miller could have facilitated an exchange of pleasantries that only proved to meet a shallow and prescribed set of criteria designed by the program funding requirements. However, I found Miller to be intelligent and well read which prompted me to try to understand more of the "why" he was sitting across from me than the "how." I provided a number of open-ended questions that allowed Miller to meter how much information he was willing to yield, and then interrupted the normal progression with an unusual question to test his attention as well as to throw him off from his comfort level.

"So Mr. Miller, what was that dream that you had as boy and forgot all about because you thought it was too late to pursue?" I asked looking right into his eyes. "Mmm... my dream? You want me to tell you about my dream?" Miller asked with a confused expression on his face. "Yes! I know someone that's as bright as you was probably a bit of a dreamer when you were younger." "Tell me about that dream that kept reoccurring", I said as I leaned forward to listen.

With an almost childlike expression on his face, Miller reflected back on his childhood and began to open up in a way that revealed an intriguing but tragic past. It took him a while to get to the dream I inquired about but eventually he outlined a dream of being a great businessman like his dad. However, his businessman/dad was also involved in a number of criminal activities that lead to his death. His dad's ill-timed death left Miller to make choices for himself from a very young age.

After Miller reached a point in his recounting that seemed mixed with conflicting emotions I decided to interrupt him and redirect his thinking. I asked "Miller, with all of the experiences associated with you as a child; what would you say is most different about the way you think and behave now?" "I'm not sure why you would ask a question like that?" Miller said. In an attempt to guide him a little more, I explained to him about a man in Scripture named *Paul*. I told him how Paul had written that when he was a child, he spoke as a child, he understood as a child, he thought as a child, but when he became a man, he put away childish things. I then asked Miller the question, "Why haven't you put away the childish things of your youth?" He looked at me, paused for what seemed like a long minute and finally replied, "That's a great question! One I must admit I don't have an answer for." "Would you like me to help you find an answer to that?" I asked him as I stood up indicating we were through with this meeting.

Miller stood up and extended his hand for a handshake and I embraced his hand as he said: "I would like that if you could give me the time." "It's gonna take a journey to get there but let's do this together...ok?" I said. The resilient scowl that once seemed common place on the face of this man had dissolved into a smile that seemed to confirm that Miller was pleased with our meeting. "I'm into this! I hope we can talk again soon," he replied while exiting my office.

Miller shared a common theme of so many people that I spoke with during this project and throughout my career as a counselor and pastor. Most have stories that detail how they are struggling with temptations of their youth. What was acutely apparent with Miller and many of these participants was the truth that they had never critically assessed why they were still entertaining the *temptations of their youth.*

What is also typical of people that have been entertaining the *temptations of their youth* is that the limits of their moral barometers are often pushed so far out that they have been all but disintegrated. Behaviors entertained along with their drug of choice seemed acceptable because they had turned off the consciousness that previously screamed "Don't do this!" Now they didn't even hear the screams! Many were unaware of the degree they had become desensitized to the lewd, vulgar, violent, traumatized lives they were living. Casual sex was as acceptable as shaking hands within this community. Relationship boundaries were usually compromised when couples shared drugs and alcohol with others and eventually shared sexual intimacies with others as well.

Some had even submitted to episodes of same-gender sex while under the influence of peer pressures and chemically induced lust-filled settings. In addition to the details of the event being blurred, many were struggling with an identity crisis having engaged in behavior they never imagined entertaining before. "I don't know what I was thinking" became a routine claim for many of our members while recounting their past. However, the problem that plagued them was not a lack of thinking, it was impaired reasoning.

The emotional scars that were left in the minds of these members were often extremely complex. We were constantly confronting their moral dilemmas while being careful to not appear judgmental. For many the social norms depicted in daily TV shows are so far removed from their past behaviors that they were no longer valid points of reference. Many had concluded: "I must be some sort of freak." Regrettably, this was also an exposure for members hiding from predators that looked for people that could not blend in with social settings.

Dr. Margaret Jamal, author of "When Girls Don't Tell" was instrumental in helping women come to terms with promiscuous behaviors that had origins in child sexual abuse. She would facilitate "For women only" meetings that invited transparency and frankness that rarely occurred during mixed gender settings. Carolyn Bush and Dr. Margaret both offered counseling sessions to women seeking help to address these complex issues.

The men had similar gender restricted meetings to address sensual issues. We adapted a panel consisting of the program leaders where we fielded questions from members and discussed strategies for addressing a very wide array of relationship issues.

FORGIVENESS IS NOT AN ENTITLEMENT PROGRAM

As a faith-based organization we taught about forgiveness with regularity. However, when faced with those that wanted to escape consequences and hide behind the principles of forgiveness we would expound on our position regarding forgiveness. For example: A member that we discharged from his position as a Peer Coach said to me "Pastor, you teach about forgiveness but you won't let me continue as a Peer Coach even after I apologized." Pausing and making certain that I had his attention, I responded: "Forgiveness is not an entitlement program. We don't owe it to you like some form of unemployment compensation. It is beneficial because we will not continue to tax you for the wrong you did. However, it does not cancel the need to protect us from future problems. I forgive you, but I must also protect our program from the liability you presented by your own irresponsible behavior. That's not un-forgiveness, that's wisdom and protection" I said in conclusion.

Dr. Margaret gave another appropriate illustration regarding this subject: "If I have been unfaithful to my husband and commit adultery and he says I forgive you, but I will not have sex with you until I know you don't have AIDS," he is not treating me with un-forgiveness. He is protecting his life from the threat of AIDS."

In this Preserved for Greatness model, we would not become co-dependents facilitating addicts playing roles as victims of this disease. Most were walking in consequences for past choices and behaviors. If their lives were to improve, it was also necessary for them to accept consequences. We encouraged them about the need to contribute something of mutual value toward their journey and destiny of recovery.

Far too many addicts have come to expect that their families are to forgive and allow them to continue putting them at risk to their irresponsible behavior. In these cases, the forgiveness is to grant closure and distance for the families and liberty from the past atrocities that were done under the family banner of love and trust. Forgiveness is not to be used as an enabling tool for someone to continue causing harm to those s/he has victimized.

An essential core task for our program was to help members acknowledge the damage caused to others by their deception, denials, and manipulative practices.

Furthermore, we found that both genders struggled with residual effects of addiction that prevented them from truly giving much consideration to the effect it had on others. Bill Wilson fittingly notes in the Big Book of AA, "*Selfishness and self-centeredness...is the root of our troubles and...driven by a hundred forms of fear, self-delusion, self-seeking, and self pity, we step on the toes of our fellows and they retaliate*" (p. 62)

BUILDING NEW FAMILY STRUCTURES

Miller was slightly older than me and yet, we were able to establish a trusted bond that positioned me as a paternal figure. He and other men in the program felt totally comfortable in referring to me as *dad*. I didn't take that lightly, additionally, like other fathers, I sought real solutions to the destructive habits that my surrogate sons and daughters were struggling with. I would not be an obligatory pay check for them. On the other hand, I would give of myself sacrificially and love them without regard to past offenses.

Beyond the structure of our program walls were often very difficult realities. Many faced roads of reconciliation with family members that were severely damaged and void of forgiveness. Most admitted to the inherit characteristics of deception, theft, betrayal, and even violence they put their families through. Beginning with a new family was the only option for many of our people.

A TWILIGHT EMOTIONAL HI-JACKING

On a cold winter night I was resting at home in bed with my wife. My cell phone rang and the number was unfamiliar. Oddly, I answered the phone anyway. "Pastor, it's Joe. I know it's late but I'm in some real bad trouble. These guys are threatening to kill me if I don't come up with some money and I don't think they're playing" Joe said talking very fast and sounding scared. "I'm listening" I said trying to discern the validity of his claims. "I'm calling on their phone and they say I won't leave here alive if somebody don't bring them some money tonight. I'm sorry to put you into this Pastor but I don't know what else to do. I don't want to die" he said waiting for my response.

"What is it that you need from me?" I asked seeking some clarity about this call. Taking a deep breath and then pausing before he continues Joe states "I need you to bring this man $100.00 right now... cause I don't want to die." I paused to consider what I should do and then responded "Where are you at?" He gave me the address and I informed my wife what my plans were and she expressed her concerns. I promised to be careful but believed I needed to go.

It was not until I was in front of the building where I was to meet him that I came to terms with how dangerous this plan was and assessed my own actions as being irresponsible. If I was to be hi-jacked and murdered, it would cause a rippling effect that would change the lives of my wife, my children, all those associated with the program and more. This was not a great idea and yet, I was there in the middle of the night trying to prevent one of our members allegedly from being killed. I looked in the mirror and said out loud to myself: "This was a stupid plan!" I dialed the number, calling back to speak with Joe, and informed him that I was outside and would not be coming inside. He relayed that message to someone and I heard someone say "Go with him... if he's lying ... bust a cap in him." I accepted that as evidence of the seriousness of the threat and prepared the money he was requesting. Joe came to the car and I rolled down the window and gave him the money and said "I hope this saves you Joe, and I will be praying for you" I said as I rolled up the window. "Thank you Pastor" he said as I pulled off. "Thank You Lord!" I said out loud to myself, realizing how fortunate I was to survive this mistake.

Word got around about what had happened and a strange reaction occurred within the membership. The members were angry with Joe *and* me. In an early session I was facilitating, a member stood up and began to rebuke me "Pastor, I want you to know I love and respect you and I really need this program... but that was not cool what you did last night. Please don't ever do that again... I mean it! This program would not survive if something happened to you. And that ain't fair to those of us that are trying to stay straight," he said to me while others offered their remarks in agreement with what was said.

Panning the room, I saw that there was genuine concern about this with many of the other members. I paused and said: "I *do* appreciate your concern and agree that it was not the wisest thing for me to do. I got caught up with the all the drama and I recognize that was not a good reason to risk all that you and the others have invested in to this program - and especially my family. I will not be making another trip like that," I said humbly.

Unfortunately, Joe did not remain compliant with the program. He relapsed again and left the program before eventually recidivating back to prison.

No amount of sacrifice is enough to convert someone else's heart. If Jesus dying on the cross was not enough to change the heart of man, then certainly me sacrificing my money, or life is not enough. I learned about how dangerous it was to over-function while working with this population. I needed to stay in my lane no matter what the circumstance was.

Early in the development of this project we saw the challenge in engaging every member that entered our facility. Retention of clientele was reportedly a statewide problem. Another typical characteristic of the addicted population was that most were uncommitted. Absenteeism for a meeting or an appointment was not unusual at all for most of this population.

Valuable resources that had been scheduled and made available would miss their mark if members would lose interest and not come to the facility. Too much time and opportunity was lost during in-take stages of members entering the program. Often they were not personally engaged with the classes and/or peers and would wonder off during a break and never return. Cost constraints made it difficult to bring in more staff which prompted innovative methods. Dr. Margaret Jamal was instrumental in designing the program we were running and suggested that we hire *members* that possessed leadership skills to work as *program aides.* We learned more about Peer-Based leadership and implemented an internal search for *Peer Coaches.*

Announcing that we were interested in finding candidates that could be hired as Peer Coaches had an immediate impact on the morale within the program. We composited a job description and printed it out so all could see the type of workers that we were looking to hire. We stated that training was available, but only the very best candidates would be selected for these positions. These positions would be contract positions without health benefits or paid sick or vacation time.

It was also expected that many of these members would not sustain long enough to warrant making them employees. Payment would occur twice per month and Peer Coaches would be responsible for managing their finances in order to retain their positions. Attendance issues were dealt with on an individual basis but intoxication, chronic tardiness or absenteeism would not be tolerated.

We shared our vision for the growth of the program and the impact needed to manage that growth. In fact, we made it clear that Peer Coaches were essential in shaping this culture. We taught how their past trials had uniquely prepared them to acquire the perseverance and character needed to fulfill their most intimate hopes. We would continue being as *hands on* as we had been, but they would be an extension of our outreach to the members even beyond the doors of our facility.

We also made it clear that no member was to ever arrive at this site and go through the morning without being engaged by a Peer Coach. These Peer Coaches were to be careful to avoid over functioning and promising beyond their abilities. They were to remind members that they were not counselors and each would refer members to staff in order to address issues that were beyond their scope of abilities.

Peer Coaches were there to help them quickly adapt to the culture. Each received a list of new members they would be responsible for assisting. They were to help them navigate their schedule of classes and to intentionally help them to fit in to class settings. They were also to intentionally encourage their participation in classes as well as to intercept any one that might present a *clear* negative influence to them.

The position proved to be invaluable. Each of the hired Peer Coaches recognized they were on ninety (90) day probations and so their behavior was exemplary. A few found out that they were also being scrutinized by other members that were not selected. There were plenty eyes on them and we needed to mentor them regarding how to handle the pressure. Our participation numbers increased as well as our reputation for having an impact program. We continued building leadership competencies with our Peer Coaches and most were thankful for the experience to learn the skill sets we were developing in them.

A by-product of this training was the insight we received from the Peer Coaches about the struggles our members were facing. These were not just text book experiences. This was straight from the trenches and those experiences proved to be priceless. There was an altered existence that operated behind the masks of program compliancy and our Peer Coaches helped to uncover it.

Loneliness also proved to be a resilient barrier for members to overcome. Some members were experiencing loneliness in the midst of crowded rooms.

Peer Coaches intentionally engaged the members that appeared to be slipping into symptoms of loneliness and submitted recommendations for counseling sessions. I will address this barrier with more specificity later on in this book.

An inherent characteristic of innovation is the unforeseen that must be conquered. We remained flexible and made adjustments as new challenges formulated.

ESTABLISHING GROUND RULES OF SELF-CONTROL

One of the most multifaceted challenges in a mixed gender program is to control past patterns of "dating" within the membership. The emotional roller coaster ride that often accompanies "dating" serves as a trigger for more destructive behaviors leading toward relapse. We set the policy loud and clear to our members: "This is not a dating center!" We implored members to work on themselves before adding someone else to their personal mess.

To help battle urges of a sensual nature, we advised some of the men to look at the female participants as "little sisters" and that helped to build healthy protective instincts toward them rather than sexual instincts. Paternal-like positions were more fragile and complicated with father-daughter type relationships because most of the women had experienced some level of childhood sexual abuse. Tragically, there was also a need for each of the male staff to avoid providing heroisms that set up unrealistic expectations from female members.

Re-victimization was a constant consideration because of the fragile nature of our surrogate family structure. Sexually inappropriate behavior from a leader could set back progress for months, years, or in some cases cause irreparable damage.

We gave multiple teachings about how lewd conversations that referenced sensual details from past incidents were often powerful mental triggers. Many people that were trying to put that life behind them found lewd mental triggers as difficult to resist as watching someone partake in their drug of choice. The sensual appetite is never satisfied and will never push away from a table of opportunity. It is a familiar partner to compulsion. Most of the people that had a longer history of substance abuse were on guard for stories that detailed cravings but appeared non-resistant to the stories detailing sensual episodes.

A young woman I will call *Cindy* had a huge appetite for attention. This appetite was consistent with most of the participants. She appeared somewhat emotionally raw in that she would frequently cry in the midst of her personal testimony stating her regrets about her previous episodes. "I hate feeling lonely... but I know I ain't ready for no relationship!" she would say.

Cindy would openly share experiences of "having dates," another way of referring to prostitution, while she also claimed she was desperate to be restored to her family and a "normal life." "I want to stop! I need this help in the worse way! I'm serious! I can't keep doing this" Cindy would shout with tears streaming down her face. Her passion appeared genuine and unpretentious. Unfortunately hers and similar testimonies also provided a provocative lure for any sexual predator that would try to tap into the vulnerabilities confirmed by their testimony.

Early one morning, I walked in to monitor a peer-led session that had already started. This was a mixed session crowded with men and women. Some of the participants were there for the first time. It was not uncommon to find new people nodding from a previously sleepless night during this session. However, the room was unusually quiet and people appeared unusually attentive. At the front of the room was Cindy sharing a testimony. Some of the details she shared were of an encounter with one of her dates. Her description was rather graphic and I interrupted her testimony to poll the temperament of the room. I asked how many of the men in the room were experiencing lustful thoughts triggered by Cindy's testimony. In that most reports targeting sexual thoughts are under-represented, I saw enough hands to conclude that this style of testimony, left unchecked, was counter-productive. I suspended the testimonies until we could provide some practical guidelines for all of the meetings that allowed for personal testimonies.

I had no evidence that Cindy intentionally engineered a high-jacking of the thoughts of the men in the room. Still, the results of the poll I took demonstrated she had triggered lewd thoughts, and by her presence was adding imagery to the acts outlined by her testimony. She had grown comfortable rehearsing the stories and rarely experienced opposition to her openness.

Manipulation and deception are almost second nature to most struggling with addiction. I was mindful of the probability that some might be tempted to exaggerate their stories in order to position themselves as "special" or more interesting. No amount of attention seemed to satisfy them when they were given the floor.

They would go on and on and on until they were cut off because they enjoyed being the center of attention. As a remedy to this practice, we gave special guidance to peer leaders about the controls that needed to be in place in these sessions. We emphasized that testimonies should focus more on their recovery paths. Giving voice to triggers only complicated the process of renewing their minds. As the senior gatekeeper to the content they received while at our facility, I would take responsibility for censuring the testimonies or at least setting up the guidelines.

As much as we labored to identify and remove the predators, there were always those that went undetected by the leaders within the program. These predators would make their move on their prey whenever they were allowed to gain the ear of a female without the protective eye of a peer leader or staff personnel. We posted a rule that prohibited romantic relationships outside of the married couples we had in the program. We also gave countless talks about the dangers of trying to manage the dynamics of a relationship while struggling to gain control of their lives.

Regrettably, we failed to effectively address the social voids in the earlier stages of the program. These voids became even more pronounced in the wake of their sober consciousness.

WITHIN THE RECOVERY TRENCHES

I heard the same concerns from people I was counseling. In a meeting where testimonies were being shared, I overheard a number of details that appeared insatiable to the majority of those listening. There was no request for the person to move on or restrain from being so graphic. It was as though some were living vicariously through the testimony. I considered this to be counter-productive and interrupted the peer-led session to bring caution to the style of testimonials.

Words are powerful and potentially paint imagery that is very difficult to remove from your mind even if you want it removed. I pointed to the talk-radio shows that incited so much fear that people began to jump out of windows. Their instrument of communication was only words. Many of the people tuning in were not tuning in for entertainment but for life saving information. However, the entertainment was unwittingly used to trigger a level of fear that was tragic.

I continued to share with them the importance in remembering that the goal of these testimonies was not to add notches on their ego-belts for the dirt and decadence they participated in. This goal should be to point to the victories they discovered or the help they still desire. I finally concluded that unless they were more responsible in the words used and the details of their past, they would continue to be used for evil rather than good and would further awaken their own appetites for vices.

Immediately following that session I had a private counseling session with a participant that admitted enjoying the testimonies given even if some of the stories were exaggerated. I expressed to him that if temptation was not desirous to us we would not have to resist it. There is nothing wrong with acknowledging that someone is appealing to you. It is your actions that follow that acknowledgement that may be problematic. If I see an attractive scantly clothed woman and feel myself becoming aroused, I have not sinned. Conversely, if I continue looking and even begin imagining what sensual things I could do with her, I am lusting in my heart and therefore sinning.

I asked him if he had a plan for what he would do with himself when he was alone to reflect on the words that were spoken and he said "No." I asked if he was interested in my plan and he replied "Yes, but I didn't know you needed a plan." I shared with him that I didn't have to experience the exact same things in my past to experience an urge that set off all kinds of alarms about what I was hearing.

I also shared that my plan was to flood my mind with the Word of God and Gospel music that I found particularly helpful in drawing me closer to God and I would continue doing this until I no longer experienced any of the urges I wanted purged from my thoughts. He appeared confused because he assumed I no longer had those urges. I told him that I recognized that the urges have a lot less impact but none the less, if left unchecked, these urges have the potential to draw me away from God and my wife whom I love.

However, I also recognized that the devil was not necessarily facilitating the urges I felt. I believe that the seed of evil flourishes when we water it with lewd discussions, or sensual details. Additionally, the evil seed also flourishes after experiencing extreme stress, or depression, or loneliness, or rejection. In short, all of those emotional states highjack our minds and provoke us to retreat or want to *numb our awareness of these anxieties and tensions* with our choice of drug or behavior.

RE-SHAPING SOCIALIZING AND TEAMWORK

Moving forward, we tested a number of theories with program outings that were intended to build new reference points of social interaction that were sober and conflict free. These outings were not funded by the program and so we had to become creative in controlling expenditures.

In one socialization effort, we transported more than 50 participants on a bowling trip that allowed members to *have a ball*! Before leaving our facility, members selected teams and captains which helped to foster a healthy competiveness.

An exceptionally effective dynamic in bowling is the team-work that is required to be successful. Each team had a level of parity with regard to experience but the primary goal was always to have fun. We occupied about 8 lanes and facilitated an elimination round where the highest team score was declared the champions. There was a contagious atmosphere of encouragement, mentoring, laughing, and celebrating that was in most cases a "first-time" experience.

"Come on man! You can do it" said many of the shouting members. In the aftermath of gutter balls you would hear "That's alright… you'll get it next time" as many applauded the effort. I recall one of the members that I will call *Al* steadying himself as he studied the bowling pins. His team was trailing but Al was hopeful that he would make a "strike!" He makes his approach down the lane and then lets the ball go. The ball is spinning toward the gutter but heading along the right side. Suddenly the ball breaks toward the center pin. It's a strike! Al begins his hilarious celebration dance which prompts the membership to shout "Go Al… Go Al… Go Al!" This happened over and over again with many other members.

Often there were multiple victory dances happening simultaneously. It must be noted that these chants and comments were not scripted! There was genuine compassion being shared even in the midst of a competitive atmosphere. I have witnessed college and professional sports that did not show as much sportsmanship as these recovering members displayed. We were truly proud of the positive social connectedness they were demonstrating.

There were no incidents of lewd behavior, arguments, taunting, fighting, or sneaking off to get a drink from the bar that was monitored by Peer Coaches and staff. As an added caution, I spoke to the manager of the Bowling Alley to request that no one associated with our group be allowed to order from the bar. At the conclusion of the event, as I settled up with the manager, I inquired about the members ordering and he confirmed there were no orders of alcohol requested. That was a good report.

We loaded up the vans to transport the members back to the facility and the excitement was still very high. There were extraordinary testimonies of how this event had effected their view of entertainment and each other as a whole. "I never knew I could have that much fun and be sober" stated one of the members. "I felt like we could win even though I never played before! I really loved the way it felt to be applauded every time I knocked down a pin" said one of the female members. "I think this helped us to grow closer together! I wanted everyone to win" said yet another member.

Fortunately, this outing only cost about $500.00 and it facilitated at least 50 members. That is a fraction of the money that many of them were accustomed to spending in an outing with only a fraction of that sized group.

Additionally, empathy and team building skills were highlighted and celebrated as we viewed a video recording of the outing. Even the recording was spearheaded by one of the members. There was much growth to our collective social intelligence. Most were amazed at the quality of enjoyment they experienced without being intoxicated, while others went forward in planning more outings that could further demonstrate this phenomenon.

Affirmation and team work seem to be a great by-product of the outing rather than a formal exercise. Mutual praise and teamwork temporarily filled social voids within the participants and increased the value of the overall program for weeks after the outing.

Another impressive result of our attempts to deal with the challenges with socializing beyond the program was our in-house news-letter. Our news letter was composed and edited by a member I will call Mr. Gun, who also supervised the use of the computer lab. There was a monthly vote for the "Member of the Month" that they also initiated. The notoriety and celebration of the "Member of the Month" proved great for morale. Many of these members began to demonstrate more awareness of their behavior and intentionally participated in a way to gain the approval of other members.

LIVE CONTENTLY WITH LACK AND PLENTY

One of the most essential elements of recovery is to learn how to adapt to the volatilities of life. The target must be contentment and not happiness. Sustained "happiness" is unrealistic and impractical. Happiness is only recognized in contrast to norms that are less satisfying. The norms of life include contrasting seasons of lack and plenty, sick and health, strong and weak. We must learn how to journey through those seasons without returning to plans of escapism associated with addiction. Defining sobriety as "a level of contentment without addictive remedies" was among our earliest principles. We do not believe that a glass of wine will necessarily send you to a spiraling course of drunkenness once you have regained your self-control. However, the compulsive urge to over indulge must be combated through a well constructed support system.

"Trouble don't last always," but it *will* come. Paul wrote about this to the church of Philippi.[7] *"12 I know what it is to be in need, and I know what it is to have plenty. I have learned the secret of being content in any and every situation, whether well fed or hungry, whether living in plenty or in want."*

---

[7] Philippians 4:12 NIV

Some have grown so entrenched with their discontentment that they fail to recognize the contrasts. They only see the negative.

Among the most common triggers we needed to address was the area of discontent. Many of the members would only focus on what they did *not* have rather than appreciate what they were fortunate to have. The past is usually remembered with a fondness. But if you challenge them to scrutinize the past, what you often unveil is more discontent. Most would agree they didn't like the people of their past or the drug of choice all of the time.

Re-learning to appreciate simple interactions, songs, beautiful weather and games were necessary but challenging for members that were so entrenched in discontent. For example: a member might complain that someone is talking too much but have nothing to talk about themselves. S/he might say that things are "*boring*" but when asked what would be *exciting* they would have no alternative ideas to offer.

They appear to see the world as somehow responsible for entertaining them even if they seem to be unwilling to engage with the world. We found that discontent dwarfed the emotional and spiritual growth of members. When the majority of their focus appeared to be on self-gratification, they seemed to be prime candidates for a relapse. Regrettably, even "getting high" would not work out their discontent.

Additionally, the discontented member may be cynical and critical of other's physical features. "She's ugly" or "I can't stand that fat #$*@*!" or "That's the dumbest idea I ever heard" are among the things we could expect to come out of the mouth of some discontented members.

Consider the following; in one situation I had driven to the parking lot of our facility and parked my car. Before I could get to the door of our suite of offices, I was greeted by a discontented member. "You the one in charge of this program" he said sitting outside on the curb. "I am the director of this program. My name is Pastor Jamal. What is your name" I said but not sure what was to follow. I was just trying to start my day off on a positive note. "I'm Stanley. This is a dumb program" he said, shaking his head to express his disapproval. I recognized that statement as a loaded challenge for me to defend the program. "Why do you say that?" I said pausing to speak to the young man. "It just *is*! I been here aaaallll morning and there aint *nothing* to do" Stanley said standing up. "What brought you to our program Stanley" I asked trying to get a baseline of his discontent. "A stupid policeman busted me for some weed and the judge said I had to come here or go to jail ... but this is just boring" he complained.

"Did the judge tell you that we were supposed to entertain you" I asked him looking for evidence that he was listening to me. "Naw, but I thought I would at least be able to do *something*" he complained again. "There is plenty you could do Stanley, but since you're the one that got busted, maybe you should listen to some people that the judge thought could help you," I said opening the door to walk in.

"They're boring" he said prodding me to defend them and the program. "Who is your Peer Coach?" I asked, assuming he had been assigned to one. "Miller, but he's boring too," He said following me in to the building. "If you think this is boring, you should spend some time in jail. Would you like that?" I asked ignoring his prodding. "Is that supposed to be a threat?" he asked with a tone of irritation. "You are mistaken. I don't need to threaten you *or* entertain you. We are all willing to help you, but that's only if you want our help," I said in a firm but cordial tone. "Well when am I gonna get helped? They aint doin nothin" he accused. "I suggest you find Miller and ask him how long it took him to get help when he first came here. If you are still not satisfied, then let's see if we can find another place to help you," I said pointing toward the room where he would most likely find Miller.

 Stanley continued with his attitude of being discontented and eventually found himself in trouble with some of the leadership. There was a written recommendation to discharge him from the facility. I met with Stanley to discuss the pending recommendation and was surprised to hear Stanley pleading with me to give him another chance.

"Why should I do that Stanley?" I asked looking unimpressed with his pleading. "I've been kicked out of everything I ever joined. School, my mother, everyone eventually kicks me out," he said tearing up and appearing to be sincere. "What are you willing to do to prove you're worthy of another chance?" I asked while I was writing on a paper. "I'll do what you tell me do. But I can't get kicked out of here. Besides, my P.O. said he would violate me if I got kicked out," he said expressing his frustration. "You can begin with a written apology and we will discuss that with the rest of the leadership" I said standing up and opening the door to leave. "He took my folder, I don't have anything to write with," Stanley said shrugging his shoulders. "Well I guess you don't have a folder then. I will let you use some paper and a pen, but I suggest you use it well," I said closing the door behind me.

We decided to give Stanley another chance but his behavior appeared to be chronic and we did not have enough resources to dedicate to someone that required such high maintenance. Eventually, we did have to discharge him due to his habitual patterns of non-compliance. However, we also made note of his behavior and tried to examine how to better use our resources to help members that suffered from *chronic discontent.*

Discontentment poisons your mind and dreams into a resolve of perpetual negativity. The cynicism that accompanies that discontentment repeals the very support that could help you.

"When one door of happiness closes, another opens; but often we look so long at the closed door that we do not see the one that has been opened for us." **Helen Keller**

Discontentment may have its roots in the broken promises of your youth. However, if you do not prescribe a new set of lenses to look through at life, you may be framing a destiny of hardships and despair for the rest of your life.

Great men experience their greatest successes after experiencing great disappointment. These great men reach for more than the possible. They reach for the impossible and refuse to look behind for a reference point or acceptance.

Contentment is not a plan of surrender but of serenity. Discontentment brings such noise to your mind that there is no peace or balance. Discontentment is as a tsunami of negative energy that targets joy, hope, and optimism. We must resist mirroring the negativity of opposition, or attempting to escape the pressures of life's consequences. We all have to face our mountains.

"Great spirits have always encountered violent opposition from mediocre minds." **Albert Einstein**

CONTAGIOUS DISCONTENTMENT

In an attempt to present personal transparency I must admit that I found myself overwhelmed with fielding discontented attitudes. For example: Late at night my phone might ring, (as it often did) and on the other end of the call would be a distressed voice of someone that is pleading with me to do something. "Pastor Jamal, they telling me that I can't come back to the program because of something I didn't even do. My roommate stole some of my stuff and I just tried to get it back and they wrote me up for fighting" said the caller. "Did you go to the proper leadership to report this?" I asked, already tired but trying to show empathy as well. "I told, but they don't ever do nothing. They said I need to be able to handle my business... so I did, and now they wrote me up" the caller says. "Well I don't think there is much I can do tonight but I will make a call tomorrow. I will update you once I talk with the right person." I said trying to assure the caller I was not blowing him off.

The next morning I would wake up thinking about the caller and start getting into my advocacy mode to try and help out one of our members. The problem is that in getting too close to the discontentment of members, my reasoning skills were impaired and the fact that most of these members are less than honest most of the time was not part of my thinking.

I called up a friend I will call Paul who is the CEO of one our partnering housing providers where the caller was a resident.

"Paul, one of my members called me and told me that he is being written up for something he didn't do. If your people can't protect the residents, they shouldn't be written up for defending themselves," I said expressing my irritation by the alleged write up. Fortunately Paul is a tolerant friend that responded to me as someone that was forgiving what I should have known rather than talking to me as an idiot. "Now… Pastor Jamal, are you coming to me with a complaint that came from a client? …Because my residents know better than to even approach me with some ole mess. They go through my staff and if my staff is in need of some guidance, then I step in. But it sounds like you're calling me like you have a problem with my staff and it's based on what a member said" pausing and then continuing he asks … "You *do* know they *lie*… right?"

Recognizing that I was not respecting the processing structure Paul had in place by taking this straight to him I said "Paul you are right, and yes I know that they lie sometimes and this might be one of those times. I apologize for not even giving your staff an opportunity to address this matter internally. I also apologize for reacting without thinking this through and investigating the viability of the story. Maybe I'm just tired. Again, I apologize Paul," I concluded hanging up the phone from the embarrassing call.

Pleading "*foot in mouth*" disease may get you a pass once but it probably won't do much to prove your competencies among your peers. I made a similar mistake after getting involved with someone that appeared to be victimized by one of the program policies of DASA. This time I wrote an email to a senior management person making sweeping charges of incompetency among DASA's staff and stated how I had expected better because of how we had proven ourselves.

The most *unfortunate* thing about an email is that you cannot un-send an email once you click on the send button. I had my doubts about whether or not it would be received well, but again I was too close to the discontent and allowed that discontentment to be my own testimony. Furthermore, I presented that discontentment without regard for the person I was sending to, the position they held, and the difficulties they were facing in running this and the other 50 programs they were managing.

I got a call back rather than an email reply and the call was not a pleasant reply. The rebuke was warranted and the situation I wanted to address was only made worse by an unsuitably worded email.

There was no point in going back to the "victim" that I was supposed to be rescuing. He had not requested the wording or the process I chose. It was *my* email, and the consequences were properly directed towards *me*. Regrettably, I could share more examples but frankly they're embarrassing and not pleasant to reflect on.

My lessons eventually cultured were to rest my mind and cleanse my heart from residual build up of discontent before making a call or writing an email. As a leader I must establish a healthy distance to apply objectivity. Moreover, I must undo contagious influences that infect my judgment and misrepresent the good work that is being done by all the parties involved.

I believe that discontent is infectious and its side effect of "Foot in mouth" disease can tank a career or relationship, while leaving a bad taste in your mouth and those that received your ill placed words. I am still trying to make amends for discontent I claimed as my own.

THREE RULES FOR LUST

Another fundamental characteristic of an addict is the focus on self-centered needs and the demands for what s/he wants when s/he wants it. This characteristic would prove destructive to any well-designed relationship even without the added burden of a compulsive behavior or addictive substance.

We would also laboriously teach about how the neurotransmitter "dopamine" that is created in the brain during lust-filled sensual encounters was similar to the chemically induced dependencies they were recovering from. Relapses were unavoidable. We drew parallels to the short lived, momentary incidents of euphoria that sex offered while costing them irrevocable consequences that they could spend a life time paying for.

However, to borrow from an old adage that says *"When the penis gets hard, the brain grows soft,"* it is pointless to intellectualize the morphing experience that occurs when passions are high and hot.

We changed our strategy and tried using the inherent authority of Scripture, pointing out there were no Scriptural teachings encouraging us to negotiate with urges that led to sexually immoral behavior. I illustrated that biblical instruction concluded three responses to those facing temptation as it relates to sexual immorality: *Run, Flee and Avoid.*

A popular 60's movie entitled "Lost in Space" had a robot character that would shout in response to attacks from aliens, "Danger, Danger, Will Robinson! Danger" This is a fitting picture to hold in your head when facing lust as it relates to sexual immorality.

Lust is identified as a core corrupting agent that we must strive to escape: 2 Peter 1:4 - 7 (NKJV) *"..., having escaped the corruption that is in the world through lust. 5But also for this very reason, giving all diligence, add to your faith virtue, to virtue knowledge, 6to knowledge self-control, to self-control perseverance, to perseverance godliness, 7to godliness brotherly kindness, and to brotherly kindness love."* In this reference, Scripture warns of the need to develop competencies of knowledge, self-control, perseverance, godliness and empathy after having escaped the corruption of lust. Without these developed competencies our attempts to avoid relapse are short lived at best.

On the other hand, if the members were confident that they were ready to commit to monogamous relationships, we offered couples counseling to guide them through the unexpected changes of relationships. Scripture also states: [8]"it is better to marry than to burn *with passion."* Whereas, we were not suggesting quick marriages, we were also not endorsing casual sex or minimizing the challenges surrounding burning passions either.

Additionally, periods of sobriety did not seem to improve or deter based solely on relationships. At the same time, it appeared that relapses were inescapable for relationships that were undefined, uncommitted and stormy.

WHEN WE FAIL TO RUN, FLEE AND AVOID

A young Black woman I will call Linda entered the program turning the heads of a number of the men in the program. She had an impressive amount of charisma and presented herself with a great deal of confidence. Dave was one of the veteran members that had proven his character enough to be hired as a Peer Coach. Dave noticed Linda and was quite clumsy in hiding his attraction to her.

---

[8] 1 Corinthians 7:9 NKJV

Having a relationship was *off limits* but clearly there was some fireworks happening from Dave toward Linda. We began to hear rumors of them spending time together and all of the staff began to keep a watchful eye on the two. They both behaved cordially while in the program setting. However, I heard of rumors that they were planning an assignation to explore these sparks that were developing between them. I talked with Dave and cautioned him because his job was on the line if what I was hearing was true. He assured me that there was nothing to worry about, but I remained skeptical of his explanation about the interactions between Linda and him.

After a *normal* weekend passed without too many fires to put out, I came in to our office to find that Dave was missing. I called his home to speak to his mother. Dave was living with his mother and there had been numerous attempts of her trying to prevent Dave from relapsing. I did not get an answer from Dave's phone and called the mother's line instead. She answered and I immediately knew something was wrong. "Good morning! This is Pastor Jamal. Is Dave home?" I asked his mother. "He's here but I haven't spoken with him for a couple of days" she said sounding rather concerned. "He didn't answer his phone. Is everything alright?" I asked. "If it was alright he'd be at work... right?" She said in a tone confirming that I needed to do something. "I'm on my way if that's alright with you" I said to her. "Come on. You're probably the only one he's gonna let in there anyway," she said. "I'll let you in when you get here," she concluded as she hung up the phone.

Our Operations Manager and I loaded up and arrived as quickly as we could. My Ops manager had a history as well and I relied on his discerning power to guide me while dealing with the Peer Coaches. Careful not to be easily turned away and yet, not too aggressive, I rang the bell. Dave's mother answered the door and let us in. "He's up those stairs toward the back" she said pointing the way. I knocked on the door respectfully and announced myself. "It's Pastor Jamal Dave. Can I come in?" I asked waiting for a response. He did not answer but I heard some scurrying in the room and so I persisted. "I know you're in there Dave, you want to open the door" I expressed letting him know I had no intention of leaving without talking to him. "Pastor Jamal? What you doin here?" he said sounding like he was stalling for time. "Let's not play games Dave. Why don't you open the door man, or I'm coming in," making it clear that he would have to face us. "The door's open," he said.

We opened the door and saw that Dave was disheveled, unshaved and a bit disoriented. "I'm not gonna jump to any conclusions. I want you to tell me what's going on," I said to Dave. Looking down and then away, as though he was searching for some words he said "You were right Pastor. You told me not to get into it with her. I did... now I'm all messed up."

"This is not the time for an '*I told you so*' speech but when did you last use?" I asked while looking straight in his eyes. Hesitantly he said... "Bout half an hour before you got here" he said, shamefully looking away. "Is there any more left?" I asked. "Nope, or I probably wouldn't have stopped," He said still not looking at me.

"You need to get your things together and go with us. You got family that loves you and we are willing to help," I said to him. "Let's go" I said holding my hand out to him. "I can't face them right now Pastor," he said with his hands still in his lap. "Everyone has an opportunity to make the best of a bad situation. This is your window of opportunity. You need to take advantage of this," I said knowing that the effects of the drugs were probably impairing his reasoning skills. Dave refused to go with us and did not come back to the facility for weeks.

When we came back without him there was very little information that we could share with the membership about what we witnessed. It was not a successful rescue mission. However it confirmed our concerns about relationships between members.

Word got around that we had actually gone to the house in an effort to bring Dave back. Members talked about how they felt about the lengths we would go to help a member. It was very different in contrast to other programs. We continued to guard against the dangers of members dating one another but interestingly, this became an easy example of the consequences that threatened their walk of sobriety.

IMPLEMENTING THE P4G RECOVERY PROGRAM

We were fortunate to have a wide array of expertise within the membership that shared their skills with one another. Some had previously worked on major construction projects and contributed new benchmarks for skill sets. These members did not look down on the unskilled men that were just trying to learn how to do something. Instead they mentored one another, offsetting the deficiencies that each of them shared.

One of the members shared that he had been a project manager previously with a crew of more than 25 on most projects. This member had fallen into addiction and was humbled by the depths of failed relationships and financial ruins he was navigating through. "I'm good with my hands. Just not so good with my head" he would share with me. However, his challenges were typical of most people that had extensive use of narcotics. His cognitive skills were compromised and when you are building things that have to be constructed within a specific level of integrity, there is little room for compromise. There is a right way to do things and a wrong way. The margin of error is narrow and it can cost lives if situations really go wrong. That is true about many professions.

Something as simple as measuring the length and width of a 2x4 required a level of accuracy that was very different than the routines of measuring the ingredients of a favorite mixed drink or monitoring how much cocaine you just snorted up your nose. We needed to re-wire the thinking process of these members to *respect boundaries*. Measuring was taught as an extremely important responsibility that all had to respect. Each member had to be trusted to measure and cut with accuracy in order to frame one wall. Failure to be consistent with that standard produced something ugly that would not stand the pressure of more walls being formed along side of it. This *principle* of measurement proved to be a life lesson that was transferrable as well.

Pastor Brady hired a member that turned out to be an extraordinary leader. This young Mexican-American, I will call Mike, was a model of integrity and perseverance. Mike was a carpenter and quite resourceful in several skilled areas. Mike had come to us with problems with addiction just like the others in the program. However, his humble spirit and love for his family framed a heart that was easy to lead on this recovery path.

Mike didn't need a lot of convincing to remain compliant. He only required guidance. Mike was no stranger to the challenges of living in the fast pace of Chicago. Mike lived in Humboldt Park. This was one an often violent, gang infested, drug territory that held a large Hispanic population. However, Mike's gentle demeanor often led us to forget where he came from. A husband and father of 3, Mike was determined to get his life back together. He was also generous with his skills. He mentored a number of students to learn the basics of carpentry and would often supervise projects that were held off-site. Among the strongest characteristics Mike displayed was his work ethic. He never cut corners or gave excuses. He was dependable and took pride in all of his work. Pastor Brady adopted Mike and his family and became their pastor and friend.

Many of the participants remained with the program for more than a year beyond funding requirements and guidelines to remain connected to the core resources, meetings and peers. Mike was one of those members.

OUR MOST VALUABLE WEAPON

Ironically, what proved to rank among the most impacting program services we offered was our Transportation. Our membership participated in an internal survey targeting barriers to their attending the program. We discovered that geographical distances were not the only challenges facing our membership. Most did not own cars or have access to anything other than public transportation. Chicago ranks among the best public transportation systems in the nation. However members would have to travel through territories run by rival gangs, drug dealers, and a variety of risk factors to continue coming to our facility. Some would have to spend hours traveling back and forth. That was too much time, danger and distance for them to risk while coming to our program.

Our program was budgeted to pay for bus passes however, even using the passes were problematic. The bus passes positioned the members as targets because of the monetary value associated with the passes. Furthermore, it did not solve the problem of too much time spent getting to our place. Our facility was only 10 miles from the heart of the city but it could easily take more than an hour to get there on public transportation.

We experimented with a small transportation company that agreed to pick up people from designated places near their homes or apartments. Unfortunately, that did not prove to be as reliable as we needed. Far too often, we had instructors and resources waiting for members to come that were late because of logistical challenges with the transportation company. Imagine this: "John Brown" gets word from a peer that our program is ideal and he would really like it if he tried coming. John arrives at our facility but has to be screened and assessed to qualify for the program. He completes the screening process and is assigned a Peer Coach and a schedule of classes. He is told to wait for a van to pick him up at a corner on the route that is near his apartment. He realizes that according to his schedule he will be gone for the whole day.

He gets up unusually early to prepare. John grooms himself with the limited amount of resources he has and heads to the corner to meet the van. John is cautious about the corner he is standing on because he does not fit the profile of most of the people that are up that early standing on the corner. Several squad cars drive by and give John a *close* look, letting him know that they *were* watching him. John tries to not look suspicious but feels like all eyes are on him standing on this corner. He doesn't have a watch and the only phone he has is the land line phone in his apartment. He asks someone passing by for the time because it feels like he's been standing there for a long while. Still, John has to be careful because he doesn't want to draw too much attention to himself. John's probation officer has already warned him that if he gets picked up one more time he will be violated and sent back to jail.

Paranoid that he would be violated again John heads back to his apartment to call our facility and asks what happened to the van that was supposed to pick him up. The administrator gets the call and forwards the call to me to let me know that someone is claiming they did not get picked up.

In the mean time, we have been coordinating the classes and resources consistent with John's schedule to make sure that he gets everything we promised him. I am calling contract instructors to make certain they arrive on time for their scheduled classes and giving them an idea of the number of members they should expect.

Alarmed that even more members may be waiting for a pick-up that has not arrived I call the driver. He says that he is running late but traffic is really bad now and is not sure how long it will take him.

We reschedule time slots and recognize that some classes may have to be cancelled because of the delay. The contracted instructors that set aside time to train on that day are not happy because they are not getting paid for classes that don't occur and they spent money on gas to get to our facility.

The van finally arrives and only has *5 members* in the van. I ask what happened to the others that were scheduled to be picked up and the driver shrugs his shoulders and says, "They would have made me too late so I didn't go." Frustrated that the driver made that decision without even telling us, we began damage control with the members that were left by phoning them and apologizing for the mix up. We reschedule for the next day of classes and promise to correct the problem.

John is frustrated and complains "I could've been picked up and violated waiting out there for that van and he didn't pick me up!" Understanding his frustration I apologize and vow to do my best to correct the problem. As a result of this driver deciding not to pick up seven members we are over staffed for the number of members we have to serve. Additionally, we will not be able to bill for the hours that would have paid the staff for their time. I hope you are getting this picture.

Seeking an alternative that was within our budget was crucial. I personally advocated for more money to be allocated toward the transportation and was unfortunately denied. There were all types of budget concerns but transportation didn't have enough service providers trying what we were trying to get their people to their facility.

We considered how vital busing strategies were for engaging students in other schooling situations and began working out options for leasing our own vans. We finally settled on a strategy of leasing multiple vans that would provide door to door service for our members. This was without a doubt the most effective enhancement that we implemented in our program. Because we were able to control when members were picked up, we could also more effectively plan for their arrival and we adjusted scheduled classes accordingly.

There were numerous by-products of this service that were invaluable. Among the most appreciated was the fact that we could offer an extended level of commitment for partners that were providing housing for our members. Most recovery houses had curfews and hourly constraints that residents had to comply with or face being discharged from their facilities. The fear of being homeless was a serious threat to most of our members. "The street is a mean place to have to live," expressed one of our members. "You almost have to use some kind of drug just to keep from killing yourself out there" he said, explaining why he could not get kicked out of his recovery home.

When we assured housing managers that we would be responsible for dropping the residents back off at their facility immediately after our program was over, most were interested in working with us. When they witnessed the other improvements in behavior, sobriety and job skills, they were even more interested in partnering with us.

Leasing the vans also opened up a number of employment opportunities for selfless, dependable drivers as well as a transportation supervisor. Among the most noteworthy was our transportation supervisor. This position required someone that was meticulous enough to organize the shortest routes to pick up people from all over the city and in some cases the suburbs. Additionally, this person would have the leadership skills to manage drivers that were seriously underpaid to perform a job that provided no days off and had extremely long hours. Most important to this position was someone that had a heart for the members that viewed this service as their life-line to recovery. We found such a person that I will call Ms. L.

Ms. L was only about 5'4 but had a big voice with a big heart, a hearty laugh, and would fight through anything and anyone to get to "her people" and she would often say "I love you and there ain't nothing you can do bout that."

This feisty woman had a history of her own and knew what it felt like to be left behind and forgotten about. She had been sober for years but understood what it meant to struggle with addiction.

Ms. L had an empathic ear and the patience of a counselor. She maintained a reputation for being encouraging to members and drivers, but let them know that she was not to be taken lightly. She had rules you'd better follow or suffer the consequences. But even for those that suffered the consequences, she was forgiving and would often advocate for someone to get another chance.

Each of the drivers had cell phones and Ms. L would be in their ears from early in the morning till very late in the evening. But most loved her and she loved them. I requested that the drivers play only gospel music and that no one would smoke on the vans. Ms. L was a smoker but stayed in compliance with the no smoking rule. She knew that if they saw her smoke on the vans then everyone would smoke on the vans. That was another area of sacrifice she took on without complaint.

There were far too many stories about Ms L and the "Transportation Ministry" she ran to put in this book. However, one noteworthy rainy morning, while Ms. L was driving a group to the facility, she had an accident. This was rare for Ms. L because she really was an excellent driver. Fortunately, no one was hurt and we experienced the advantage of leasing a van as opposed to buying it outright, because the leasing company brought a van out to her location and Ms. L was able to continue picking people up that day. She demonstrated her resilience to keep going and her humble spirit as she apologized about twenty times for her part in the accident. Later she expressed how thankful she was that our first concern was for *her* safety and for the members on the van. "They love us here, and you should never forget that" she would say to a crowded room of members waiting to go back to their homes.

Each of the providers had to contribute to the combined salaries for theses position and all were in agreement that Ms. L was our MVP. Ms. L would spend countless hours mapping out routes and connecting with members that relied upon our vans to participate in our program. Everyone had to log in their contact information with Ms. L because the one certainty you could count on was if you were in the program and needed a ride, Ms. L would send someone for you or come herself.

Our transportation became the engine for our program and helped to set us apart from most of the other programs in the state. Our drivers were noteworthy as well. The position was a coveted position. However, it was extremely demanding. Some drivers were willing to drive all over the city picking up and dropping off members and then take public transportation to their own residencies before they retired. Others would park in the parking lot of our facility and then have to drive back to the facility to get their cars before going home. Admirably, these drivers expressed being willing and happy to do this.

Imagine getting up at 5:30 to get ready to go get a van and then drive that van along a previously planned route to pick up a maximum of 14 passengers and bring them back to the facility where scheduled classes are waiting for your passengers. Then imagine that after all of *that* driving, turning around and going to get more if need be.

Chicago was notorious for having horrendous traffic jams. It was an ongoing challenge for all of the drivers to navigate through extreme levels of congestion while trying to keep schedules. In addition to that challenge was the moody personalities of the members that were riding on our vans. Some of the members viewed the vans as "off-site" and so they thought it was appropriate to do whatever they wanted.

Extending program rules to the vans was difficult because the drivers would often have to enforce those rules. On some routes there were Peer Coaches that would assist in keeping order but occasionally there were the routes where the driver had no assistance in controlling the behavior on the vans.

During one of the many trips back from the facility there was a great deal of heated conversation happening on one of the vans. It appeared that this had escalated from something that had occurred much earlier in the day. But under no circumstances was a driver to allow fighting to occur on his or her van.

The driver of this van was Mike. Mike was not known for being outspoken and confrontational, but he could see that something was brewing in the back of his van. Mike tried to diffuse the arguing by turning up the gospel music but they just shouted louder. Mike told them they needed to calm down but the emotions were far too high and they did not have an ear to hear.

Mike pulled the van over and pulled out his cell phone making a call to me. "We got a mess going on out here

Pastor Jamal" he said to me. "They look like they want to fight. Should I tell them to get off the van?" he asked. "Mike, it's your van and you have the authority to put anyone off the van that will not comply with the rules" I told him. "I got your back. Do what you need to do Mike."

For what was probably the first time ever, I heard Mike raise his voice. I could hear the arguing going on in the background but then Mike shouted "Hey! I got to finish my route and you can't fight on this van. Either sit down and stop or get off this van." "You can't put us off this van" said one of the arguing members. "I don't have to because I got the keys. If you start fighting, this van ain't movin. If you get off the van to fight you ain't getting back on. It's up to you" Mike said holding up the keys demonstrating his control of the situation. They both looked at each other and thought about their options. Neither wanted to walk from where they were and neither had money to pay for public transportation. Without any more words they moved to different seats in the van and refrained from arguing. Mike put the keys back in the ignition and started the van. It was the first time that members got to see the leveraged authority these drivers had. Mike continued the route and there were no further incidents to report on that trip.

On an entirely separate incident, we experienced an unprecedented situation that affected everyone within the program. We were always aware of the fact that many of our members were dealing with a variety of serious health issues. However, we had never developed procedures for handling critical health problems that might occur on the vans.

During an otherwise normal morning, I got a call from one of the drivers. With a great deal of emotion and fear in his voice, one of the drivers said... "Pastor, I think he's dead... He just fell out... I don't think he's alive." One of the members had experienced either a heart attack or stroke and it happened while being transported to our facility on one of our vans filled with other members.

Scripture tells us "*...you do not know what will happen tomorrow. For what is your life? It is even a vapor that appears for a little time and then vanishes away.*" James 4:14 NKJV

Death has a way of making an imprint on your mind even if it happens to someone you don't know. However, when it occurs to a "family member" it has a way of touching you in a very different place in your heart. This was a member that many had seen grow from an angry and distant person to a laughing and "good to know" peer that we all loved.

This member had just recently expressed how glad he was to be in this program because he was finally getting his life together. To see his lifeless body as paramedics came to examine his body and confirm his death was traumatic and it hit home in the hearts of everyone in the program - even those not on the scene.

Immediately I contacted the state project director for the program to inform him of what had happened. He said he would initiate the paper work required but would be awaiting our detailed report of the incident surrounding this death. I reviewed the deceased member's folder to see who he had indicated as a family contact person and made the call to inform them of the tragic passing of their son.

As a pastor, I had often comforted loved ones after the sudden loss of a relative, but this one felt very different. Several of the other pastor/providers gathered in the main meeting room with the membership. We knew that there would be a wide range of emotions that they were facing and it appeared appropriate to deal with those emotions together rather than individually.

We approached this meeting more like a memorial for the member than a debriefing. There were a number of testimonies shared about how they felt about this member and other members express their concerns for the brevity of life. "He was sitting right there yesterday, and now he's gone" said one of the members as tears began to form in her eyes.

Death is a reality they were all too familiar with, but this time it did not appear to be related to their lifestyle choices. This appeared to be "his time to go" and it came very suddenly and unexpected. *"a vapor that appears for a little time and then vanishes away."*

THE GOLDEN RULE – LOVING ONE ANOTHER

Another noteworthy member was our Peer Coach supervisor whom I will call Ben. Ben shined as someone that was very experienced with the recovery culture. We would often rely on his sharp nose to sniff out deception in a story that just didn't add up. He was also rather skeptical of the program in the beginning, but became a believer as he witnessed how authentic our love was and our ideology proved effective.

Late one very cold night I got a call from Ben. He had dropped off one of the members at a facility that served the homeless. They met at a church and during this trip Ben met a number of people that were interested in coming to our program. Ben was doubtful of their eligibility but wanted to know what I was willing to do to help them. "It's cold out here Pastor. I know they're not in the program but tomorrow morning these guys are going be kicked out on the street. What do you want me to do?" he asked waiting for an answer. "Find a way to schedule a pick up for them and let's bring them to the program and see how we can help" Ben said. "Really? That's ok? I mean these guys carry everything they own in a bag. Is that alright?" he asked again as though he was testing me. "You have to keep things in order but find a way to make it work. It's alright. Make it work" I said trying to let him know I fully supported his request.

Ben arranged for a pick-up with Ms. L and then looked in our storage area to find some storage cabinets. These were executive styled wardrobes and blended well with our décor. Ben used those cabinets to store the bags of the people he arranged to have picked up. These homeless members had even less advantages than most of our membership. Most had hygiene challenges as they rarely showered or washed up. None had food or money to buy food. However, they found even more compassion as our members pooled their lunch money in order to buy enough to feed them as well. Our church food pantry was able to contribute toiletries to help with the hygiene.

This was one of many transformative lessons that our members were afforded to learn. [9]*"It is more blessed to give than to receive."* Unfortunately, some go through life without knowing what it feels like to give sacrificially for the good of someone else. Most people have heard of the "Golden Rule" but have no idea of what it really looks like. The Golden Rule is known around the world in secular and religious settings: *"Love your neighbor as yourself."* This is cited in at least ten different places in Scripture. Clearly this was

---

[9] Acts 20:35 NKJV

universally accepted as a humane and appropriate attitude to have for centuries.

In light of that statement, I am confused as to why these members that were among the neediest were also among the most willing to give to these that were homeless. It appeared as though these members had a greater capacity for love and generosity while in the midst of their struggle than some people who were affluent and "stable." I am not making a broad indictment on all of the wealthy. However, I am stating that Ben and those members that gave out of their *lack* were experiencing "*the better thing.*" Their selfless, non-judgmental acts positioned them as part of the solution. An act that was restorative regarding their character. An act that proved these members were valuable assets to their community.

We found this and other examples of our members demonstrating selfless acts and becoming part of the solution essential in developing attitudes of independence and self-respect.

[10]"*Real self-respect comes from dominion over self, from true independence. ... Interdependence is a choice only independent people can make. Unless we are willing to achieve real independence, it's foolish to try to develop human-relations skills. We might try. We might even have some degree of success when the sun is shining. But when*

---

[10] Seven Habits of Highly Effective People – Stephen Covey Pg 92 IBID

the difficult times come -- and they will -- we won't have the foundation to keep things together".

PATCHING UP THE CRACKS - G.E.D CLASSES

30 years old and sitting in a room with other adults, admitting that you could not read, or that you had failed to develop basic math skills was an incredibly difficult thing to do for any adult. However, when you add the level of secrecy that usually accompanies addiction it becomes even more difficult.

We enrolled men and women, Black, Latino, and White that failed to graduate from High School or acquire their G.E.D. Some of the members were still in their teens and others were adults with teens of their own. All of these members had somehow fallen through the cracks.

It would not be fair to blame all of academia for the reasons these members failed to assimilate the same curriculums that the majority of the other members and all of our staff had completed.

On the other hand, conventional methods of teaching these adults were not going to prove effective in our program. If you combine the time constraints governed by program budget caps and the wide range of gaps in learning as well as the inherit challenges in re-engaging with structured learning models after dropping out, you have a very challenging job on your hands.

Our first partnership was with Triton College to handle this area of instruction. However, their instructors were not used to dealing with the wide gaps in learning we were faced with. Eventually, they withdrew from teaching the G.E.D. classes.

We needed someone that had the empathy of a pastor, the organizational skills of a grammar school teacher, the patience of a mother, and the leadership skills of an officer in the military.

From the pool of leaders that went through the R.A.T.E.S Certification training, we found an energetic entrepreneur that was running Breakthrough Academy; Mrs. Candra Chavda. The students affectionately called her "Ms. C." This was a bright young woman that had a background as a teacher, an athlete, a model, an actress, a business owner and an incredible heart of compassion. I do not have the time and space to properly frame the dedication and impact that "Ms. C" offered to this program, however, omitting the contributions that were connected to the hope framed within the G.E.D. classes is just not an option.

I had organized G.E.D. classes for adults previously. However, the risk factors associated with these students were so vast I knew I was way over my head. Ms. C. helped to develop curriculum and structure that engaged the students, nurtured them along, assessed their progress and motivated them to learn what had previously escaped them.

Initially, Ms. C designed a pre-test to determine the gaps in learning that needed to be addressed in order to develop targeted curriculum. Tragically, after reviewing the results of the pre-test, she discovered that the goal of initiating a G.E.D. class was not practical. She came up to me with a look of frustration all over her face. "I need to talk to you" she said looking like she wanted my complete attention. "OK, what can I do for you Ms. C?" I said trying to let her know I wanted to comply with whatever program-related request she was going to ask me.

"There is no way I can prepare these members for G.E.D. when some don't have basic grammar skills, or math skills and some can't read. We need a Pre-G.E.D. course" She said with so much conviction I didn't even think about challenging her findings. "Considering the time constraints we have with them, do you have a plan to do that?" I said anticipating her response. "I have an idea, but this is going to require some investment and I need to know I have your full support" she said while letting me know she was not playing. "You have my full support. But we don't have much room in the budget right now. I just need you to let me know what that support will cost so I can do my best to try and make that happen. Can I count on you updating me?" I said extending my hand so we could shake on this plan. "You can count on that once I figure it out" she said as she stood up to walk out the room as though the meeting was over.

Ms C. was not upset with me and I knew that. She was challenged however, because she was in unchartered waters. My job as the C.E.O. was to make sure she trusted I would not leave her on those waters without a paddle. Ms. C was a very passionate and committed woman. That was good news because working with the challenges associated with the members of these G.E.D. classes were extremely difficult and these students needed someone that would be willing to fight for them. Sometimes she also had to fight through patterns of quitting developed over years to keep her class coming. Retention levels were a difficult challenge for each of the facilitators. Ms. C. convinced her students that she was committed and dedicated to helping them and they needed to show up for her if they expected her help to continue.

Some of the students might have been late for the early sessions but they would show up for their G.E.D. classes. I would greet a student in the hall way "Glad to see you this morning. What happened to you earlier?" "I wasn't gonna come today. I had too much drama goin on... but Ms. C. don't play! I got to get to her class" the students would say as they pushed through to get to the class. It always made me smile because I knew that motivation was something that Ms. C knew how to give. She also gave a great deal of love to her students. Most of her students spoke of her with love and admiration and rarely challenged anything she instructed them to do.

Another key component for helping to build an effective recovery path was to address the low self-esteem associated with the failed past of our members. Ms. C. offered "Image" classes that addressed hygiene, fashion and image. She taught the women how to behave as proper ladies and how to put on makeup. She even facilitated a make-shift spa that helped women to view themselves as beautiful and "special." For some of the women this was their first time ever experiencing a spa. The smiles were priceless and for many, their lives were changed from that day going further. She also helped the men to groom themselves and even arranged to bring in clothing from second hand clothing stores. Rarely did she ask to be reimbursed.

Ms. C. would sometimes bring correction to a male member that was talking to a female member in an inappropriate manner in a way that prompted a quick apology: "I'm sorry Ms C." "Don't confirm you're sorry. Apologize to her!" Ms C. would say. Her position as teacher was very instrumental in educating our membership into pursuing and embracing better images for themselves.

The stigma associated with addicted populations often foster feelings of insecurity and worthlessness. That attitude is often demonstrated in their posture and the way the population dressed. Most are trying not to bring attention to self because they fear being exposed. Once they become accustomed to hiding their looks, their health, and behavior, it is not difficult for them to become indifferent to fashion or grooming trends.

Fortunately for the members, there were several that were skilled in cutting hair. Some had previously worked as hair stylists. Shaping the image of our members was not just an inside job. We were addressing the outside as well. "You only get one chance to make a first impression" became a valuable motto for those seeking employment or those that were hoping to move beyond a scarred past.

Staff members would often contribute to a fund that would be used to compensate the stylists who would occasionally cut hair for a small fee of $10 per head. Most were willing to cut anyone's hair for free if an interview was pending and they were short on funds.

We witnessed incredible cosmetic transformations within our membership that encouraged them to continue their recovery paths. We took group pictures with members and staff and there were few that could distinguish between them.

We were careful not to facilitate more "dating" but seeing the smiles on members that were previously without hope was precious. We took pictures of them and posted it on break room walls so that they could be reminded of "good times."

It was 8:30 AM and members were scurrying around trying to get to a mirror and fix their hair and makeup. There was a buzz going around. Vans were fueled and lined up outside to transport the majority of our members to one of a many job fairs. Some were examining their folders where they held their resumes. Others were role-playing with other members and staff to prepare for the imminent interviews they were about to experience.

For some, this was the first time they were preparing for an interview in years. For others it was the first time ever. "All hands on deck" was the instruction for all of the staff. We needed every staff person to focus on the preparation of these going out to this job fair. There was much at stake. Getting the job was not the only consideration for this outing. For many, just getting to the job fair was a major accomplishment. Making certain that others were able to handle rejection was also a concern. Rejection could be a dangerous trigger to retreat and go back to previous negative behaviors. Scripture prepares us for challenges like this: [11]*"...count it all joy when you fall into various trials, [3]knowing that the testing of your faith produces patience. [4]But let patience have its perfect work, that you may be perfect and complete, lacking nothing."* These were lessons we shared over and over again to off-set implicit despairing thought patterns.

---

[11] James 1:2-4 NKJV

We coordinated a time for our membership to arrive with the Job Fair coordinators because there were so many in our group. Our staffing helped to look over the membership's clothing, grooming, resumes and greeting lines for their interviews. It was show time and all of the staff was as anxious as proud parents sending our children off to school.

"Let's go!" shouted one of the drivers indicating it was time to load up the membership. "Wait! We didn't pray! Somebody has to pray before we go out there!" said a number of the members. A brief prayer was offered asking for calm, safety, and favor with the perspective employers and the collective excitement of the room was transferred to the vans waiting to transport them.

This group hit the doors of that job fair and infused the place with energy, confidence, and with such polish and professionalism that there were a number of members hired on the spot. The organizers of the job fair announced we had an open invitation to any event they sponsored. This outing was a notable success!

In reflection, there were so many contributions to the progress that was represented in this outing that I must apologize to those that have not been recognized in this accounting. All of their efforts were essential and without the synergistic contribution of everyone connected to the program we would never have witnessed the transformed lives celebrating this successful outing.

Another pivotal part of the program happened in the vocational classes where many of the members learned skills in web searching for employment opportunities, keyboarding basics, basic word processing, carpentry, cable installation, electrical wiring, cable installation, painting, framing and even dry wall.

Pastor Brady, C.E.O. of Brady Has a Bunch Ministries, facilitated much of that training in conjunction with Apostle C. D. Bush of Maranatha Church. Both provided the opportunity to develop employable skills using their hands.

Often when you are trying to instill disciplines and new rules to govern the behaviors of members, it is helpful to engage them into workshops that have clear cut rules that manifest short term results. Some of the men had no previous experience in any of the areas being taught. However, most were convinced that they needed to learn something other than the skills they used to sell drugs, or engage in criminal activities.

The ability to work within a group on a single project was also therapeutic for the students. This was a safe work environment because no one was allowed to smoke within the facility or engage in drinking during the program. Emotional outbursts were controlled through the prohibited use of profanity and hitting while on our property.

Everyone was working on a recovery path and there was a mutual respect for one another that crossed ethnic and cultural backgrounds.

In addition to these services, we collaborated with other service providers for Recovery Housing, and Mental Health needs as well as other clinical needs that were beyond our capacity to provide. Methadone was an acceptable remedy, according to CSAT/DASA, for members struggling with heroine addictions. However, we never endorsed, recommended or distributed any medications to our members. Our focus was strictly Recovery. Some of our participants remained connected with 12 step programs patterned after Alcohol Anonymous in order to remain compliant with probation guidelines from the court system.

In contrast, our program structure was unique to any AA 12 step model or NA (Narcotics Anonymous) model of recovery. Our structure resembled a social/vocational training setting. While we integrated Scripture within our training, we also built curriculums that targeted sustained sobriety as the goal. Some models express a perpetual dependence on a system. Ours targeted transformed independence that matured to empathic interdependence.

It was a warm spring morning about 11:00 AM. The computer lab was packed with eager members that were trying to develop computer skills. Ignoring the heat and sitting in the middle of the lab was a young man I will call Larry. Larry became a star student with the most improved statistics of any person starting the computer class.

Conversely, when Larry first started going to our program he was referred from one of our collaborating agencies. He was a well mannered young man but unfortunately he rarely participated in any of the sessions he attended.

I interviewed Larry to assess the range of services he needed in order to acquire some level of employment. Larry had no employment history to speak of and more importantly when I asked him what he knew how to do he said; "Sell drugs!" I looked at him and asked "Is that what you want to do?" "No, but I don't know how to do nothing else." He said respectfully. When I asked if he had ever been on a computer he said: "Not really." I concluded the session and walked him into the computer lab.

I gave him a brief orientation about a "typing tutor" that would help him to build up his keyboard skills. He looked at me and said, "How fast do I need to go to get a job." I told him that a rate of 30-40 words per minute was a basic requirement in most settings. Larry took the pre-test and scored a rate of 2 words per minute. He looked at me like there was no chance at all but I challenged him. "If you put in the time, I believe you can get to 10 words per minute within 2 weeks." He looked surprised but accepted the challenge.

Larry attended each of the other classes that we scheduled for him but his routine was to sleep in the classes. Larry suffered with side effects from the methadone he was taking from one of the other clinics where he was receiving assistance. We were restricted from making any recommendations regarding the treatment any of our members were receiving. Therefore, our hands were tied regarding his dilemma. I explained the importance of Larry attending and participating in the classes but it appeared as though he was powerless to remain awake during the other classes.

At the conclusion of the 2 weeks I targeted for Larry's progress report, Larry walked into my office with a big smile on his face holding out a report that read he was typing at a rate of 12 words per minute! I complimented Larry for his progress and encouraged him that he could do so much better if he really applied himself in the other classes as well. "How badly do you want this Larry?" I asked him. "I want to do better than 40 words per minute!" he said beaming with confidence. "Maybe you could speak with your case manager at the clinic and see if she could make a recommendation to help you out." I said, being careful not to overstep our boundaries.

Larry left our program that evening and came back the next week with a new pep in his step. He was certainly a lot more attentive and participated in each of the classes. While in a budgeting class that I facilitated I asked for a show of hands for those that wanted to help me frame a practical budget they could live with. To my surprise, waving his hand with a beaming smile on his face was Larry! I invited Larry to help me and he offered great insights to the cost and materials that we needed to consider as well as the essentials that we needed to build a budget.

In a private session with Larry I asked "What happened to you? Where did all of this energy come from?" "I asked my case manager to reduce my dosage so I could be more alert in school and she agreed," he said revealing this contagious smile that I had rarely seen before. Again I complimented Larry for his progress and shared how proud I was of him for taking the initiative to request the necessary changes in his plan to be more alert. He vigorously shook my hand and exited my office smiling from ear to ear.

Over the next few months, Larry exceeded his goal of 40 words per minute and brought me a report that reflected a rate of 60 words per minute! This newly developed skill built the confidence and excitement Larry needed to progress in each of the classes he attended. Larry continued to overcome his introverted ways and excelled in his pursuit for employment as well.

Larry was without a doubt a great illustration of a life turned around for the good. His improvement was noted and appreciated by all of the peers. Larry was asked if he could tutor members that wanted to know how to type like he could. I approved his limited assistance and he also assisted the Computer Lab supervisor I will call Mr. Gun to keep the computers working and maintained. This new level of responsibility also assisted in keeping Larry pointed in the right direction regarding his recovery.

DEFINING COPING MECHANISMS

The paradigm shift regarding the way we should view difficult times, disappointments, devastating losses and the like is outlined in Scripture stating: "*3We can rejoice, too, when we run into problems and trials, for we know that they help us develop endurance. 4And endurance develops strength of character, and character strengthens our confident hope of salvation. 5And this hope will not lead to disappointment.*" (Romans 5:3-5 NLT) Finding the purpose and/or value for the inescapable trials of life is antidotal to becoming frustrated or depressed. Numbing the pain caused by difficult times may complicate the matter and exchange pain for addiction. I am convinced that it is essential to find a coping mechanism that brings you comfort when life appears unbearable. To be sure, it does not have to be –and *should not* be -an addictive substance.

In one of the meetings I offered a challenge to the members to sing the lyrics to a song written by Hezekiah Walker. I had printed copies of the lyrics for each of them.

The lyrics are:
I need you, you need me. We're all a part of God's body.
Stand with me, agree with me. We're all a part of God's body.
It is his will, that every need be supplied.
You are important to me, I need you to survive.
I pray for you, You pray for me.
I love you, I need you to survive.
I won't harm you with words from my mouth.
I love you, I need you to survive.

I led the group to sing along with me and observed a transformation that was truly heartwarming. In this room filled with people from a variety of cultures, families, financial and educational backgrounds were men and women that were affirming their need for one another. Men that were otherwise scowling and disconnected were embracing other men and women while we sang this song together. Tears began to form in the eyes of most in the room and these were tears of joy not sadness. Members that had previously argued within the same day had set aside differences in order to participate in this wonderful ceremony of love, encouragement and acceptance.

One of the most powerful lines in this song is the line "*I won't harm you with words from my mouth; I love you I need you to survive.*" Too many of these participants had first-hand experiences of people that had gossiped about their failures. With all of your money and dignity gone as a result of your addiction, your reputation is extremely fragile. The promise to not harm someone with words from their mouths appeared invaluable in framing the new trusts within this group. Trusting people become more trustworthy than skeptics.

This was just one of the songs that we used to cut through feelings of distrust, bitterness, hopelessness, depression, anger, and more. Music has long been acknowledged as a universal tool for unifying people from different settings. In fact, I would go as far as to say that no program, drug, book (*other than the Bible*) or supplement is as effective in breaking through what appears as impenetrable barriers than music.

Companionship and "sponsors" are extremely helpful in lending essential guidance in moments of crisis. But no one can be with you at all times. We all need those coping mechanisms that can remain available to us even when everyone else is elsewhere or unavailable. I have found my relationship with God to be faithful and powerful and music to be consistent in leading me through my most difficult moments.

I have used music to cope with countless difficulties in my life; even when the difficulty appears to be more about me than anyone or anything else. Music has been used for thousands of years to address tormenting elements of life. In 1Samuel 16, Scripture tells us that David used a harp to relieve King Saul of his distressing spirits. It reads that Saul was "*refreshed and well*" after David would play his harp.

In addressing my own battles with distressing spirits today, I rarely select from today's most popular artists. The art of composing a well placed note, a harmonious chord or tasty melody and lyric appears far too infrequent in many of today's popular songs. I personally prefer to listen to the musical artistry from great artists such as Nat King Cole, Keith Jarret, Bill Evans, Dexter Gordon, Luther Vandross, Fred Hammond, Israel Houghton, Jean Carne, or my Aunt, the late Abbey Lincoln to name a few. I am careful to choose appropriate genres and lyrics to listen to, because some music genres and lyrics can intensify the negative feelings you are struggling with. It could prove disastrous to listen to favorite songs you shared with a previous lover. The emotions triggered by that song could be overwhelming and set off depression, anger and even hopelessness.

Classical music such as Bach's Aria, or Bethoven's No.4 in B-flat Major can frame a peaceful ambience for meditation and prayer without the dangers of lyrics that might paint vivid imagery of past relationships.

Gifted to play piano, I have also been blessed to accompany my very talented wife, Dr. Margaret Jamal, whose voice and personality have often provided the best accompaniment for a brief retreat from life's challenges. Dr. Margaret, an accomplished vocalist is quite versatile in her range and genre of songs she composes and performs. Whether we are playing and singing songs of a gospel, jazz, or pop genre, music is a healing balm for our mind, body and spirit. Music is also an extremely effective coping method for people of all walks of life.

A young man, I will call Lil' Pete who looks 15 years older than he is, rises from his seat in the back of the room. His clothing is not color coordinated, reflecting designer tags and is oversized to intentionally cover the mammoth sized wounds that cover his life. Lil' Pete is strategically positioned in the back to minimize as much contact as possible for fear of exposing the stench attached to his body that hasn't seen a shower in weeks. He pulled back his hood that was covering his hair that desperately needed to be introduced to a comb or hair cut. He pauses awaiting his turn to speak and works up the courage to speak. Acknowledged by the leader positioned at the front of the room he says: "I don't know why I am still here after all the wrongs that I've done. I should've been dead! I'm not even sure that I'm happy about the fact that I'm not." Lil' Pete says, sitting down and pulls his hood up again attempting to reduce his visibility for scrutiny.

With escapism being the major motive behind much of the compulsive addictions, it is sometimes frustrating to them that death has not rescued them from their perilous lives. It is not logical to them that they could ever make amends for the volume of pain they caused to loved ones and strangers alike. Death appeals to them as a logical resolve and retribution for what has happened.

Cultivating the emptiness that plagues so many like this young man into something that is selfless and fulfilling was imperative. Our efforts had to be intentional and tracked for future intervention strategies.

Months later, another young man that was fairly new to the program stood up and declared that he would have taken his own life if not for the help he received from Lil' Pete. "I didn't know if you realized how much I was hurtin', but you never quit on me man. And the next morning when I wanted to end it all, you showed up at my door and kept bangin till I opened the door. I never thanked you for that, but I just wanted to say *that* in front of *everyone*... Thank you Lil Pete! For bangin through the noise I had in my head!"

The need to give recovering addicts purpose for their lives is often inseparable from the need to stay sober. This need is best facilitated in their actively helping others to sustain a life of sobriety. The persistent banging of Lil' Pete was more effective in aborting a suicidal attempt than the program activities were. Lil' Pete was not even aware of his usefulness but this young man described his persistent help as a life saving effort.

This type of support is framed under the heading of Peer Based Support. Some reject this level of support, citing the liabilities associated with peers relapsing as a result of well intentioned attempts of intervention. We experienced some of that within our model called *Preserved for Greatness*. But the same liability exists for the trained professionals in this industry as well.

As a safe guard to the liability associated with peers, we reserved Peer Coaching positions for members that demonstrated a sustained sober "experience" navigating the vicissitudes of life and recovery. That "experience" is not acquired through academia but framed by specific trials, perseverance, and character that all of us were uniquely equipped to survive.

HERE COME THE JUDGE

Among the collaborative partners that stood up and stood out for their passion about addressing this problem of addiction was Judge John P. Kirby. Judge Kirby had a task force that included our agency as well as representatives from TASC, the Police Department, the States Attorney's Dept, The Board of Education and several other agencies. This task force brought a valuable dynamic to the membership's understanding about the court system they previously believed was stacked against them.

The Judge and his task force collaborated to seek viable solutions to offset the number of people that were going to prison due to non-violent drug related offenses in

Cook County of Illinois. His diversion programs and optimism provided a model to pave the way for reform within the court system. The Judge also advocated for the additional resources needed to engage defendants in educational programs and vocational skills.

I witnessed the Judge show leniency to non-violent candidates that he believed had a reasonable chance at responding to the resources of our task force. Sentencing alternative strategies did not always yield the results that we all hoped for, but the fact that there was a Judge advocating for people that would otherwise receive prison time was encouraging to the membership and our staff.

Judge Kirby and his task force visited our facility and observed some of the workshops, GED classes and role-plays that we used to prepare our members for employment opportunities as well as sober life-styles. They expressed how impressed they were with the progress of our membership and were even more encouraged to send us more worthy candidates.

In a day and time when minority communities often express a great deal of distrust for the police department, attorneys and the court systems in general; Judge Kirby's task force was a bright shining alternate star.

It is commonly accepted within the substance abuse community that until a person truly wants stabilizing sobriety for themselves their addictive issues will continue and sobriety will be short lived at best. However, I find it counter-productive to continuously define oneself as an addict. One of the most liberating Scriptures I found in my life was "*17 Therefore, if anyone is in Christ, he is a new creation; old things have passed away; behold, all things have become new.*" 2 Cor. 5:17 - "*all things have become new*" answers every area of shame and guilt. Redefining yourself to the stigmatized label of addict seems to serve those that are capitalizing or benefiting from the addiction rather than the person reinventing themselves and breaking free.

If I introduce myself to you as a recovering burglar, would you continue listening to me explain how *recovered* I am or would you immediately start considering how to avoid inviting me to your home? We live in a label-intensive society. When someone identifies him/herself as a doctor you feel something entirely different than if someone introduces her/himself as an ex-felon. The doctor may even be less trustworthy than the ex-felon, however, in this current society you are taught to trust the doctor and to be skeptical of the ex-felon. The same is true of a recovered addict.

Rarely do we know how many years of service the doctor has behind his title, nor do you know what her/his patients would say. However, the societal acceptance markers rank him as trustworthy rather than someone with similar levels of competencies if there was a background of drug abuse.

If all things have become new, then why would I continuously identify myself by the past markers I no longer have? Maybe I should because of the re-occurring urges and thoughts that enter my mind. Maybe I should because of the amygdala highjack that occurs whenever I recognize that I am approaching the same type of social settings that I frequented when I was completely lost. In my mind I may hear "Danger Aaron, Danger!" But *I* would see that as a helpful warning and change directions. What about you?

Those things may never stop repeating. Conversely, if you have developed the disciplines that frame your consistent resistance to temptation, and leverage your strength with God, a support group and/or sponsor, then why would you continue to define yourself by the past behavior?

While facilitating a workshop in job-readiness/interviews, I addressed a group of young men and women that were each frustrated with the social tag of "ex-felon" they were forced to include on every employment application. The consensus was clear and unwavering; they hated being stigmatized for a crime they paid for by doing their time. Noting that the U.S. was the only place that had that practice, many felt hopeless unless the practice was barred.

It is also noteworthy to applaud the efforts of Congressman Danny Davis for championing the Second Chance Act that has helped to address this barrier for ex-offenders. On the other hand, the fight continues as marginalized populations continue to try to amplify their voices and pleas for fairness.

Most of our membership had co-occurring disorders that needed attention from the mental health community as well as the substance abuse community. However, they wanted nothing to do with additional stigmas that would follow any documented treatment.

If there was ever an opportunity to offer the authority of Scripture to correct mis-information it was in that meeting. I shared the verse of Scripture Ephesians 5: "[8] *For you were once darkness, but now you are light in the Lord. Live as children of light.*" This Scripture highlights the potential for transformation from *past* lives in darkness to *changed* lives of light. If they needed hope for a transformation from the past to the future thousands of years ago, then certainly we need it today. I continued to teach and witnessed a shift in the meeting that continued to build the most significant healing balm in a recovery plan...hope. The questions came and thankfully, I was able to facilitate answers to their questions. I empowered them with 4 words to begin a response about their past: "**What are your concerns**."

We performed role-plays where I was the interviewee and then the interviewer. When they witnessed how I handled their questions about the past they prescribed for me they were encouraged. I also demonstrated why there was no need to lie.

On one occasion, they insisted that I interview with the following background: I had served 2 years in prison for a Drug Abuse Violation.

I was applying for a retail position and the abbreviated interview went something like this:

"Good morning sir, my name is Aaron. Thank you for seeing me and giving me an opportunity to answer any concerns that are not clear within the resume I submitted to you." "Good morning Aaron, my name is Mr. Johnson. I reviewed your resume and I can see that you have a number of skills that are important to this position, however, I also see that you have a gap between the date of your last listed employment and now. Can you explain that to me?"

"I most certainly can Mr. Johnson, but can you tell me what your concerns are?" I said.

"My concern is that I don't know what you were doing during this period between your last employment date and today" said Mr. Johnson.

"Well let me clear that up for you. I have been actively seeking the latest trends and competencies for the retail industry so I can be better prepared for my next

opportunity. In short I have been studying Mr. Johnson,"
I said looking him straight in his eyes.

"And where have you done this studying" asked Mr.
Johnson. "Wherever I could; sometimes I would read an
article on line, or in a book, or listen to a training video
or maybe even ask a store manager if he or she could
spare a few minutes so I could ask a few questions. Does
that address your concerns Mr. Johnson?" I asked
watching him study my application.

"Well... Yes. But...what about this box that's asking
about you being arrested" He said pointing to the
application.

"Well Mr. Johnson, I would be glad to answer your
questions, but it would help me if you could tell me
what your concerns are." I said, as though I was eager to
address his concerns.

Mr. Johnson began to squirm as though he was a little
uncomfortable with my responses. Rather nervously he
said "Well... I am concerned about hiring a criminal that
would rob me blind... if you know what I mean..."

I nodded affirming that I knew, saying "I think I do Mr.
Johnson, and let me assure you that the charges brought
against me had nothing to do with your concerns. I am
not a thief and I would never steal in any situation
especially from the employer that is paying me a wage.
Does that address your concern Mr. Johnson?"

"Well Aaron...you... didn't really tell me what the charges were" Mr. Johnson said with a raised eyebrow.

"That is correct Mr. Johnson; because the charges were not relevant to your concerns. Is there another concern you need me to address Mr. Johnson?" I said as though I wanted to make certain I had addressed all of his concerns.

"Well how do I know your charges are irrelevant" Mr. Johnson asked shrugging his shoulders.

"Mr. Johnson I am quite aware of the fact that you could pay for a background check that would reveal the charges. In light of that, it makes no sense for me to lie to you when I know you can find out the truth on your own. However, if I can save you some money and build the trust you're looking for, then I think we would both be a lot happier. Wouldn't you agree?" I said leaning forward in my seat.

"Well yes Aaron and I must admit you did address my concerns. Why don't you give me a call back later this week and...."

After this role-play ended, the hands went up and there was a new found excitement about interviewing. Some were skeptical of the interview going so smoothly, but others thought the style was an effective style they had never attempted before. I did my best to teach them how to tailor the style to fit their personalities and from that point we were on track for many of our members to interview well with a realistic hope of getting hired.

I went on to tell them that many people were comfortable defining people by their past until you require them to speak to their "concerns." An interview is not an interrogation! Once you address their concerns it is much more probable that they will be open to see who you are and not limit you to whom you were.

Additionally, we reassured members that we were committed to helping them to interview with their new communication and interviewing skills. Daily we would perform role-plays to deal with the inevitable question about their criminal past or addictive behavior. We did our best to help members with individual barriers that blocked their chances for employment. Since many of these skills were transferrable, most were thankful and empowered to take life one day at a time hoping that this would be yet another sober day and closer to getting a job or closer to restoring a valued relationship.

TRANSFORMATION FROM THE INSIDE OUT

Without challenge, I am acutely aware of the sustainable structure required to develop new habits in order to replace old habits. We must work on ourselves from the inside with discipline and through process. Stephen Covey wrote: *"Inside-Out is a process -- a continuing process of renewal based on the natural laws that govern human growth and progress. It's an upward spiral of growth that leads to progressively higher forms of responsible independence and effective interdependence."*

I can vividly remember the faces that seemed illuminated as when a light goes on after I preached to a small congregation with all of my power "God is not trying to catch you! You've already been caught! He desires to set you free... and to draw you close!" He says clearly in His Word: *"12Draw near to God and He will draw near to you."* Maybe I am just a romantic at heart, but I get all warm inside when I picture in my mind, God almighty desiring to draw near to me. There is a deeper dimension of closeness than that of sensuality. This is "closeness" beyond what we can see, hear, touch, smell, or taste.

The balance of spiritual redemption and interdependence that is fostered through the mercy and favor of God to make us whole is awe inspiring. Connected to the purpose and plan He has for us is also the power to set us free. That power is not negated or diminished by those that seek structure or rituals to guide them from day to day. Similarly, it is not the fasting that holds the power to deliver someone of evil spirits, but the response of God almighty, Who has all authority of heaven and earth.

WHY CAN'T WE BE FRIENDS

Companionship can host a deeper dimension of contrasting emotions to fill the voids left by the harsh

---

12 James 4:8 NKJV

challenges of life. Some of the earliest recorded Scripture reads: [13]*"It is not good that man should be alone; I will make him a helper comparable to him."* If it was not good for mankind to be alone in a virtual paradise, then certainly it is not good for him or her today. Later on in Scripture Solomon declares [14]*"He who finds a wife finds a good thing, And obtains favor from the LORD."* What is implied in this verse of Scripture is that a partner worthy of marriage is a "good thing." On the other hand, there are so many that have used alcohol, gambling and drugs to address marital issues.

I have counseled more couples than I can recount and I am still in awe of the depths of ferocity and malice that some are willing to hurl at spouses. Others have all but forgotten what they promised at the altar when they said "I do." Far too many are only focused on the regrets that torment them for what they did. The volatile tempo of any marriage requires a great deal of sacrifice, patience, forgiveness and perseverance. Whenever you are ensnared by the chemical dependency of alcohol and/or other drugs of choice you develop a self-centeredness that is toxic to any relationship. The results are even more tragic when there are children involved as well.

Worth noting again is that addiction is not a terminal illness. There are many marriages that have survived addiction and many families have experienced

---

[13] Genesis 2:18 NKJV
[14] Proverbs 18:22 NKJV

restoration after recovery. Some have found the guidance needed through marital counseling or family counseling. More have sought spiritual models that are facilitated by their local church. Whatever your choice for recovery, forgiveness will play a pivotal part in moving forward.

Fundamental to the recovery process is restoring hope. Shifting the perspective about life's challenges away from a depressing failure-based assessment of life toward the development of valuable competencies has transformative results. We are making great strides in restoring hope when we point toward a redemptive value that is somehow preserved from the wreckage of years of being enslaved by addiction.

Our Recovery Class was usually led by Pastors' Dave Turnipseed and Dan Thomas. Both of these leaders helped to facilitate and engage members to give voice to their own recovery paths. Pastor Dave is noted for being as easy to talk to as he is tall. His illustrations were often humorous and able to get underneath the masks of members looking to just go through the process. Pastor Dave also worked along with Ms. L with the transportation. His personal vehicle would often be used when the vans were not available. Members would often tell stories of how intimidated they felt when this tall man, 6'6", would approach them to invite them to the program. Once Pastor Dave opened up with his hearty laugh, it was clear he was just a "big ol teddy bear."

Pastor Dan was a fiery motivator that presented passionate illustrations rooted in Scripture to turn the member's lives around. He was also very instrumental in training members about how to install cable. As a contract worker with companies like Comcast, Pastor Dan learned and taught the ins and outs of operating as a cable installer. He mentored several members so they could pursue employment opportunities.

Ezekiel 36 reads: [25]Then I will sprinkle clean water on you, and you shall be clean; I will cleanse you from all your filthiness and from all your idols. [26]I will give you a new heart and put a new spirit within you; I will take the heart of stone out of your flesh and give you a heart of flesh. NKJV

Also fundamental to recovery is admitting the things you are powerless to change and placing your hope in God, Who has the authority to do what you cannot. I am powerless to clean myself of all of my filth but there is nothing too hard for God. We are powerless to give ourselves a new heart or put a new spirit within us, but there is nothing too hard for God. Life has a way of hardening our hearts like stone. But God can give us a new heart that is able to feel compassion for others and to love without the bitterness and skepticism that once dominated our thoughts. Now more than ever, I understand why we must strive to come to God as little children.

There are few times when I feel more honored about this existence on earth than when my now seven month old grandson reaches up to kiss me. He reaches up in a clumsily manner with an open mouth that is drawling and his eyes, wide open seem to say… "I love you paw paw"… and I melt.

His motives seem truly pure and unpretentious. Who can resist an offer of that type of pure love? That pure and unpretentious heart can only come from a clean heart. That is what I imagine our God desires of us and we are incapable of presenting that heart to Him without His help. In my own secret place, I confess my weaknesses and His Word comforts me with 2 Corinthians 12:9 "My grace is sufficient for you, for My **strength** is made perfect in weakness." With my heart cleansed by His grace I am able to draw on His strength to draw near to Him and walk in freedom and love rather than shame and guilt.

DENYING LUST FOR SOBER LIVING

I also firmly agree with Titus 2: "11 For the grace of God that brings salvation has appeared to all men, 12 teaching us that, denying ungodliness and worldly lusts, we should live soberly, righteously, and godly in the present age," Even after we are taught to deny these lusts and commit to sober lifestyles, we are constantly under attack from various temptations. I presented as a banner whenever I spoke what is taught in James 4:7 "... submit to God. Resist the devil and he will flee from you." I am still confident in this strategy and yet, there appears to be a battle that is less obvious and even ambiguous regarding our submitting to God.

For myself, I found no trouble in agreeing with God about the inherent evil in certain behaviors. But, I was not clear in my role or responsibility with regard to the temptations that appeared resilient and reappearing. I understood submission as acknowledging God's authority and will for my life. However, I found it challenging to follow Him when it appeared the devil was not fleeing. I also found it challenging to resist the devil's schemes of temptation when the lures seemed to come without notice or invitation in settings that were supposed to be safe zones. I can remember experiencing lewd thoughts in the midst of singing songs like Amazing Grace. "Come on Lord! Get this stuff out my head," I would plead.

I can honestly state those thoughts happen far less frequent now. Maybe that is what Paul was going through when he wrote: [15]"...I do not count myself to have apprehended; but one thing I do, forgetting those things which are behind and reaching forward to those things which are ahead, [14] I press toward the goal for the prize of the upward call of God in Christ Jesus." His statement of "forgetting those things which are behind" has always intrigued me. The present tense of forgetting blended with that which has already been placed behind us illustrates the struggle many of us experience; especially those struggling with compulsive behavior.

Our pressing toward the goal is a daily challenge that is continuously confronting the things we are forgetting. Fortunately, we can expect that things will continue to get better if we continue pressing.

---

[15] Philippians 3:13-14 NKJV

On a spring morning, during an early schedule-break some of our members went outside and discovered there was someone in the facility parking lot that appeared in trouble. Because each of our members had a great deal of experience with "street life" they were quick to conclude that they were looking at a possible drug overdose. It appeared that the driver had come off of the nearby expressway to pull in to the parking lot in order to address the passenger that appeared unconscious and lifeless. The member's response to the scene is what was so impressive to me.

One of the members ran back into the room where I was still conversing with some of the members and shouted: "Pastor! Somebody's in the parking lot... and I think they're having some sort of an attack or overdose! Come and pray!" My first thoughts were that someone in our program was in trouble. Dealing with this population, there were times that we felt as though we were an emergency triage and needed to be ready for the unexpected every day.

With the adrenalin flowing I ran toward the parking lot and as I got closer, I realized this was a stranger that was just driving by. "Someone call 911!" I shouted. A number of our members began to gather around as I could see that the passenger was already out of the car lying on the pavement with the driver kneeling over her trying to help the passenger and revive her. Though I had basic training in CPR, I was not trained in reviving someone that appeared to be experiencing effects from either a drug over dose, or an epileptic seizure. There was no evidence that the passenger was seizing, she appeared to be breathing and so I concluded that this may have been drug related. I instructed each of our members to give them room and heard repeated shouts from the members "She needs prayer! Pray for her Pastor! She's gonna be alright... Pastor pray!" shouted members standing around. Prayer is an area where I am quite competent and I quickly agreed with them. I encouraged them to pray as well.

I approached the passenger, and the driver looked up at me with a look of fear and confusion. I kneeled along side of the car and laid my hand on the passenger's head and began to pray. One of the truly amazing things about prayer and faith is that when you have people gathered around that truly believe, there is expectancy in their faces and in their prayers. Our prayers and faith interceded for this woman and in a just a few moments she began to stir from her previously motionless state. Members began to thank God as this disoriented and dazed woman regained consciousness. She groaned and mumbled a few unintelligible comments and we helped her to sit up. I gave the driver and passenger space and made room as the local police were finally arriving. We thanked God and returned back toward our facility to discuss what had just happened.

I immediately told my administrator that we needed to fill out a report about this even though we had no names of the passenger or driver. A traumatic incident had occurred during our session and members witnessed an event that would affect them in a variety of ways.

I didn't need to prompt anyone to begin debriefing about the experience. They all seemed eager to express what they witnessed and started sharing their personal thoughts about what had just unfolded. "I knew if you prayed for her she was going to be alright." Shouted the member that ran back in to tell us what had happened. "That was good but we all prayed... remember that!" I said in an attempt to point out their parts in their stories. I expressed how much I appreciated the quick thinking they demonstrated to go and get help as soon as they witnessed someone in trouble. I also pointed out how different their responses were now from what they might have been when they first came to us. Again, this is about being able to responding in a caring manner in the midst of a desperate situation rather than running from it.

Many had already witnessed personal experiences of a member passing out in the facility and after prayer they were revived and recovered. We were less than half of a mile from the nearest hospital and yet, the person recovered before the paramedics arrived. That and other events convinced them that trusting God to help them even before the other help arrived was not a ridiculous idea. This was not about religion. This was about faith! "I thought she would die like the other men did before..." said another member that appeared relieved but still very excited.

There had been a separate event where a couple pulled into the facility parking lot and began to shoot up using heroine. We only found out what had happened because someone noticed that the driver and passenger were in the car unconscious and one still had a needle in his arm. Police responded to the scene and preliminary reports confirmed they were both dead and suggested it was a heroin overdose. As more information came through we found that there was a lethal batch of heroin that was being distributed in the neighborhood and some where calling it "good stuff" because they thought it was more potent. We had no forensic evidence about the contents apart from the heroin. However, I was certain whatever was in this batch was lethal enough to kill someone after just one "hit!"

The event proved to be a teachable moment for the membership. We talked extensively about how so many were taking drugs that they knew very little about. I recall asking the members in the room "What is in crack cocaine?" Most hesitated before trying to answer but even after allowing a number of them to try and answer the question, it was still not clear. "It depends on who's fixin the packages!" said one of the members. "I don't even know why they call it cocaine because there ain't much cocaine in the packages these days" another member said. "Do you know what is in the package?" I asked again. "A lot of dealers just use stuff from under the sink... but I don't really know..." said yet another member.

They were clearly framing the inherent dangers of buying "street drugs!" No one really knows what is in the packages. "Good stuff" was declared "good" as a result of the reported experiences from the people using it. There were no TV commercials explaining why the experiences happened or cautions about side effects that could happen if you used the products. Someone might pass out after trying a package and oddly the perception would be "that's some strong stuff... I gotta get some of that!"

There is much evidence supporting the premise that addicts suffer from impaired reasoning skills. Cognitive abilities are rarely evident in the midst of settings where people are sharing needles, having unprotected sex with people they just met, and snorting some white and powder-like substance up their nose. Among the many cautions that have been ignored in the minds of the addict is the cognitive skills that would question the contents and integrity of what they are putting in their bodies.

We hoped to educate them and to restore some of the cognitive skills they had set aside. We taught about the damage caused by extended use of chemicals in everything from cigarettes to crack cocaine. We would also address triggers that lead toward relapses and strategies that could be implemented outside the controlled setting of our program.

While framing a social connectedness that served as a new family dynamic for this group, there was an obvious gap in this delivery of service. Our membership experienced a continuum of highs and lows from their first encounters when they awoke till the last encounters before going to bed. Daniel Goleman writes [16]*"It is not that people need to avoid unpleasant feelings to feel content, but rather that the stormy feelings not go unchecked, displacing all pleasant moods."*

Our participants would often leave the program on a high note and experience an altercation on the way back to their dwelling place that would agitate their attitudes and stress levels. Most members displayed underdeveloped social skills. These dynamics contributed to the overall challenge of retention. Away from the safe zone and structured environment of the program was an earsplitting volume of conflicting lifestyles that were uninvited and yet, very present. Social competencies such as team-work, trustworthiness, understanding others and conflict management were underdeveloped and required a delivery method that was appropriate for adults and immature teens in order to manage turbulent emotions without experiencing devastation.

In our brief season of program encounters we were forced to prioritize the developmental challenges

---

[16] Daniel Goleman's Emotional Intelligence pg 57;

uncovered so we could remain compliant with program deliverables. Rarely were we given enough time to develop empathic skills of communication, influence and conflict management to matured levels. These deficiencies led to outbursts of anger and depression resulting from unchecked turbulent emotions.

Fortunately, we maintained a controlled atmosphere for the participants due to the collective intelligence of the staff members that were present. The socialization exercises that occurred off-site while unsupervised, still proved challenging for the participants.

ADDRESSING STRANGE BED PARTNERS FOR SEX

Science has shown that alcohol and other mind altering drugs impair our ability to perform in bed. They do not enhance our performance because our best performance requires our mind and bodies to work in concert. Alcohol and drugs are effective at removing moral values from our decision making process. On the other hand, why would you need to remove moral values from your decision making unless you are trying to enable your own participation in an act that is contrary? For centuries men and women have done things under the influence of drugs or alcohol or some other intoxicating substance they regretted. God remedied the notion that we should have hang-ups about marital sex. He declared in His word that the marriage bed is undefiled between a husband and his wife. What is done between a man and his consenting wife is not out of bounds in the eyes of God. However, bringing an influence like drugs or alcohol to bed is not an enhancement to your sex. We have the resources to experience the gift of sexual pleasure within us. Preserve this experience by excluding conflicting influences.

AVOIDING VERBAL HIGH-JACKING

Sitting at a traffic light on Chicago's South Side, a young woman pulled up alongside of me and without warning I was bombarded with some of the vilest and raunchiest language I had been exposed to in years. I turned to show my discuss at the lack of consideration the woman was showing for me and everyone else in ear shot of this language only to discover that this filth was actually part of a recording. A deep bass drum accompanied by some unidentifiable electronic rhythmic sounds joined in to surround this "artist" on the recording.

What was also shocking was the business suit this woman driving the car was wearing, presenting a profile of conservatism. However, the woman appeared indifferent to the level of vulgarity she was blaring from her mobile sound system. She turned and met my look and appeared surprised. "What?" she shouted over the recording. "Could you please turn that down?" I shouted back. She responded with a look of indignation and pulled off as the light changed bobbing her head in rhythm and proceeded to turn the volume up.

Extended exposure to any behavior, no matter how disgusting, raises the tolerance levels of the people that are exposed to it unless there are stronger influences that can reinforce moral standards guiding our tolerance levels of acceptable behavior.

I repeatedly heard personal accountings within counseling sessions where I was led to constrict explicit details. This was not a practice restricted to women. Men as well were just as willing to provide more details than I felt necessary to address their issues. However, vulgarity/profanity emerged most frequently from female participants.

Whenever we address the temptations and lures that battle in our minds we must also be aware of the verbal imagery that is offered without invitation and without a safety net to guard against it. We cautioned our staff to develop safeguards against the toxicity of conversations they were drawn into. Most admitted that it was a problem and agreed that we needed to plan for a time of daily cleansing to sustain healthy reasoning patterns.

I have asked other pastors about their strategies in handling explicit details including pornographic materials, a rape or incestuous relationships and sadly found most pastors either tight lipped about it or not experienced in handling this matter at all. That led me to conclude that these pastors were either not confronting these issues within their congregations or were in denial of the probability of them existing. In any case, I adopted a practice suggested by Dr. Margaret

Jamal, to quickly refer any 1-1 session that involved a woman to her or one of the other female staffed to address those issues. I knew that I needed to guard my own thoughts from any sensual high-jacking that involved another woman. Here is where we have to abstain from the mere appearance of immoral behavior if we are to continue as respected leaders.

RETRAINING THOUGHTS GONE WILD

Identifying temptations is easier when they manifest as external influences rather than internal urges. For example: It is easier to turn the channel of a program that is rated "X" than to discard an image stored in my mind not by choice but as a hijacking conversation or image that happened during a phone call or a advertisement that comes during a "time-out" or commercial that forms as a trigger.

I can also state with transparency that I have not always acted as quickly to discard that lewd or sensual image as I would have desired in retrospect because it "felt good." Conversely, this hesitancy gives evidence of a warring that is going on within my mind and members. Scripture frames the war in Romans 7: *"For what I will to do, that I do not practice; but what I hate, that I do."* However, in Chapter 12 of Romans we are encouraged to be transformed by the renewing of our mind. This "renewing of our mind" addresses the pockets of images and experiences that challenge the pure lifestyle we desire. Scripture instructs us in Philippians 4 to meditate on things that are *lovely, pure, praise worthy and of good report.* Here lies the healing balm of our mind. Filling our minds with what is pure in exchange for the things that are sinful is the transformative strategy for renewing our minds.

This is not an easy task because most people crave what they are most familiar with. It is also very difficult to continue to consume "jalapeno peppers" and still enjoy the delicacies of a scrambled egg. Many feel they have to add Tabasco sauce just to taste the eggs because their taste buds are no longer sensitive to the comparatively bland taste. The same is true for life experiences that are so spiced up with drama and lewd excitement that spending a night at home reading a good book is unbearable. Even planning to spend time dancing and dining seems too boring to endure unless combined with some drug or alcohol enhancement.

I know that God has preserved us for Himself and redeemed us for a purified life. His cleansing grace that brings salvation has also freed me from the compulsive effects of drugs. He's provided "fresh water" to revitalize my taste buds for His goodness and a sober life.

I found tangible results for what we believed was effective as well as evidence of a need to expand the knowledgebase of this compulsive disorder. We were not seeking comparatively good results. We were hoping for sustained sobriety within our target population we served. It was imperative that our services improved in substance and efficacy. Allow me to continue to give voice to the experiences that I was afforded through this project.

FIGHTING SHAME AND DENIAL

I was speaking to a large group of self-proclaimed substance abusers teaching about "overcoming the Evil within" when I acknowledged a raised hand that prompted a profound question. He said "Pastor, I got high because I wanted to get high. I don't think it had anything to do with the addiction. I just liked it. So am I really addicted or not?" I took my time in answering the question because I could tell by the silence in the room that this question was an intriguing one for the majority of those there.

I answered "If you like the way you feel while engaging in a substance that alters who you are and reshapes the moral barometer you had before you engaged in it, then we have to look at what the stronger influence is.

Is it the appetite of your "liking to get high" that is stronger or the fact that your appetite has been reshaped to an unquenchable pursuit of a first hit?" I said, pausing to allow for emphasis.

Continuing I said: "If I were a betting man, I would wager that the high you claim you like continues to fall short of the high you pursue. Is that true?" He answered

"Yes! Everyone knows you can't get that first hit again." I inquired; "then what would you call the state of mind that causes you to compulsively go after something that continues to disappoint even though you spent everything you had that was valuable to you to get it?" he thoughtfully responded... "I guess... mad that I didn't get it!" I asked "Would you do it again?" He paused and then said ... "Probably..." Convinced that he and the rest of the group was following me I concluded "So you would agree that you would continue spending everything valuable to you on something that continues to lie about what it will bring, in hopes of something you seem to never get, even though you get mad when you are disappointed...that's what we call a habit and an addiction. Would you agree with that?" Recognizing that his premise was faulty, he sat down after saying ... "I guess so."

The shame-bound disease/sin that is associated with addiction has as much to do with <u>what</u> the addict is willing to do for the drug of choice as the dangers surrounding the consumption of the drug. Over and over again we heard of the shameful acts that each person participated in for the sake of "getting another hit" and with each of these stories was a clear and obvious attitude of shame.

Additionally, shame is often the catalyst for seeking the drug in the first place. Some are ashamed of the failure they face in relationships, work, socializing, or even school. But when they seek to escape confronting those issues, the drug of choice comes with a number of strings attached to it.

The business of dealing drugs is never an honorable one. Dealers know that you are desperately seeking to escape something at great risk. Dealers also know that you are risking exposure, violence, incarceration, financial ruin and they use that card to trap you into choosing between despicable behavior and exposure. Void of cognitive skills and a moral barometer, many of our members admitted to performing unimaginable things. Once you agree to that behavior, dealers continue to use the added behavior to the threat of exposure in order to leverage their control over you.

WOMEN; ARMED AND DANGEROUS

Another dynamic that further heightens the effects of this addictive life style are the co-occurring disorders of women that have been raped and/or sexually abused. According to Rev. Dr. Margaret Jamal who serves as a pastor, author and talk show host of "My Time to Tell", the following should also be considered: "The use of drugs significantly neutralizes the moral fences that aide women in resisting their urge to use their bodies in controlling and manipulative ways. It also increases their appetite for an enhanced sensual experience." Additionally, she said "Men who inflict rape upon women unwittingly contribute to weaponizing the sensuality of abused women."

"These women who become compelled to use their sensuality to control, manipulate, and ultimately abuse their targets, find it difficult to fight the compulsion to use their bodies." Often this "weaponized" body is used to manipulate people they care about in order to get what they want. What is worse, they deceive them in order to gain things their loved ones would disapprove. Because the flesh is never satisfied, many abused women are optimal targets for addiction.

On the other hand, it is when their bodies lose their most attractive attributes in the most sensual areas of their shapely bodies, faces, hair, etc. that these women may become more receptive to receiving an intervention or a message of recovery.

In "normal" settings there is great pressure and emphasis to "look hot." The addictive appeal of affirmation that comes from both genders is real and powerful. Tragically, it rarely stops at just the lust of the eye. Recovering women that have grown accustomed to using their bodies as a weapon to manipulate and control men find it as natural as breathing to move beyond social or career barriers or rejections.

There is a desire within us that fights as a compulsive effort to satisfy itself. Galatians 5:"[17] For the sinful nature desires what is contrary to the Spirit, and the Spirit what is contrary to the sinful nature. They are in conflict with each other, so that you are not to do whatever you want." NKJV

This conflict is echoed as well in Romans 7:"[23] But I see another law in my members, warring against the law of my mind, and bringing me into captivity to the law of sin which is in my members." Fighting an external enemy as in "The devil made me do it!" is often a more appealing battle to frame in our minds than combating an enemy that is warring within our members. But what led to us getting into this war in the first place?

Again I refer to the thousands of men and women that afforded me snap shots of their lives to assess the circumstances surrounding their journey before their wars eclipsed into addiction. I found something common to each, and recognized it as a "void." There was an "emptiness" inside that framed their dissatisfaction of who they are and what they have. A relentless "noise" that terrorizes them to do something about it until they muffle that noise with some mind altering substance that diverts their thinking toward anything else or a euphoric "nothing" at all.

One of the members of our Preserved for Greatness project challenged "but you just don't understand... it felt really, really good" as a nervous laughter filled the room; "It was like... wow! "How long did it last?" I asked the young woman. "About a minute" she chuckled. "And how much did it cost you?" "About $10.00!" she replied. "Did you forget to include the cost of the despicable things you did in payment for that hit?" I asked. Suddenly, as if a flash of memories went through her mind, her demeanor changed and the rest of the room as well. She said: "I don't like to think about that." "I know it's easier to not think about that and the hundreds of ten dollar bills that followed and even worse were the things you were willing to do, but, the cost was much more than $10.00. You need to always remember that" I said.

In a counseling session I had with a young man, he shared "I don't even know when it happened but somewhere in between me trading the gold necklace my mother gave me and the first time I agreed to do stuff I never dreamed I would do... I lost a part of me... and I don't know if I can ever get it back." I assured him that there was restoration available but he would have to go through the process one day at a time. I remember telling him "You can't get this back as fast as you lost it... but if we do this right... you will value it so much more that you won't be willing to give it away again."

I also find it noteworthy to share one of the lessons we learned about people that got hired and still found it too difficult to remain sober when dealing with the most difficult person they have to deal with… "Self."

One of our peer leaders we hired was extremely competent in encouraging members in the job-readiness classes and was even leading a budgeting class for the participants when he missed a scheduled work day. His light shined brightly and so his absence was noticed immediately. We immediately dispatched Recovery Coaches to find out the status of this Peer Coach. They were skilled at finding missing participants and were very familiar with the behavior patterns and family members of most of the participants. After only a few hours they called the office stating they had found this Peer Coach and it was clear that he had relapsed. As part of our policy, they drove him to a "detoxification" facility that kept him for a mandatory 48 hours.

Upon his release he was transported to our facility where I was able to initiate a counseling session. It was crucial that this Peer Leader be assessed as quickly as possible for a potential re-deployment of his responsibilities. However, the inherent deception that accompanies addiction makes that assessment difficult. It is difficult to accept the word of even an established leader as truthful once the individual has relapsed.

Without engaging in a lot of talk, I gave the "PC" an assignment to write down the sequence of events that led to his relapse and left him with himself and a pen and paper. I told him that this was not a punitive stage but an inquiry to the level of support that was needed for him.

His honesty was required to assess the level of support he needed and this was his responsibility in this part of the intervention. If he refused the assignment we would be forced to relieve him of his responsibility and suspend him from the program for 30 days. Because our PCs were the most educated about our structure and time needed for recovery, all of them agreed to the course of actions that were required and all got the additional help that was needed.

Breaking the level of secrecy usually associated with addiction was a constant battle. Even after members were willing to admit a relapse there was resistance to disclose details they found embarrassing. In this particular case, we were forced to relieve this Peer Coach of his responsibilities and provided an enhanced level of support to stabilize his path of recovery.

In a separate incident, a young ordained minister within the leadership was drawn into an inappropriate relationship with one of the participants of the program. We began to closely monitor and to record all of the sessions and instituted a rule preventing 1-1 mixed gender counseling sessions.

I heard the wisdom of one of the female leaders to re-visit our commitment to daily corporate prayer among the leadership. Regrettably, I failed to model and implement the regularity of this practice in the face of turmoil. Whenever we hit a patch of turbulence we seemed to forfeit the scheduled prayer. We would pray individually, but clearly my mistake was not insisting that we make the time to pray as a staff. In hindsight, I believe that some of the turbulence we went through was more of a symptom of the lack of prayer rather than the volume of problem-infested clientele. However, we did follow procedure and removed the staffed minister from his responsibilities.

REBUILDING MEMBER CREDIBILITY

The membership petitioned for an open house setting that would invite the community, local politicians, family members, probation officers and other key people in their lives to personally witness their progress. Each of our program providers collaborated with membership to present dramatizations, singing, puppet shows, and testimonials to help the invited guests learn about this transformative experience that was occurring. We stated very clearly that our goals were to change their perspectives and presumptions about the value, progress and future of the membership in this program. We were confident that our program was working and could help a lot more. Additionally, we hoped they would be willing to embrace these that had demonstrated remarkable progress on the road of recovery.

Politicians, friends and family members thanked us for the showcase and expressed encouraging statements to the membership about their remarkable progress. The membership reported stories of barriers coming down within their families. One female member stated "Today, my kids love me today. My family loves me today. Today my family gave me keys to the door. I never had keys to their door before." Can you empathize with the joy of finally being trusted to come and go as you please? Empowered to come in without questions about what you want and if you are high? These testimonies were powerfully motivating to all that witnessed them.

From a community where so many of the members had been rejected and locked out of the lives of their families, these testimonies proved powerful at building hope in the hearts of everyone connected with our program.

The open house also demonstrated the independence that had been developed within the membership. Crucial to the evidence of sustainable sobriety is the demonstration of independence, accountability and compassion for others. This snap shot provided potential that is rarely experienced within short-termed recovery programs.

Underdeveloped social competencies result in poor decision making and dangerous or deadly behaviors. Similarly, in a letter to the Galatians Paul wrote [17]"...the heir, as long as he is a child, does not differ at all from a slave, though he is master of all,." What a powerful illustration of the lives of people that have been enslaved through their temptations!

The addict, in so many ways, displays the behavior of an irresponsible and rebellious child. The consequences of their failure to resist temptations adds up to far more than a "time-out' or being "grounded" for the week, instead they are reduced to adults that are not trusted to make grown up decisions in their lives. As you read on in that chapter in Galatians 4, it is clear that Paul is suggesting a shift in behavior is expected of you because of your position as an adult. That is positional leadership and accountability is part of that position. In a similar challenge Paul wrote: [18]"11 *When I was a child, I spoke as a child, I understood as a child, I thought as a child; but when I became a man, I put away childish things.*" For the addict the choice is clear; grow up and put away the childish and self-centered attitudes if you are to break free for the slavery of addiction.

---

[17] Galatians 4:1 NKJV
[18] 1 Corinthians 13:11 NKJV

So many professionals within the mental health and substance abuse community are stuck in an "Us against Them" battle about effective strategies to address compulsive and addictive disorders. Many have considered faith-based approaches skeptically and refuse to acknowledge them as credible. Conversely, the studies of neural science as well as psycho-spirituality suggest that there are more dimensions to the existence of people (mind, body and spirit). Regardless of the conflicting reports that support people that have a strong faith-based component to rely upon appear to heal better and faster, many of the secular professionals reject the notion that there is any credibility to the concept that "God" healed them.

I also found the documented results that are representative of "faith-based" approaches are sometimes limited and often incomplete. Regrettably, I also found volumes of data promoted by the mental health community that are built on assertions that have not been tested without biases to support its own legitimacy. Far too many programs have to choose a path or delivery of services that is lacking in impact, and/or sustainability for the sake of funding criteria. There is an incredible opportunity for all communities to surrender territorial lines of evidence based results in order to share and compare best practices for a mutual goal of sustained recovery and sobriety.

It is no more ridiculous to consider it a valid point that there are multiple dimensions to this problem of addiction than it is to consider that at least part of the solution may reside within a spiritual realm. At the very least it would be far less combative to simply acknowledge where both positions are valid even if there is a difference of opinion about the conclusions. I am hopeful and optimistic that the advances within effective neuroscience research will lead to finding common ground and bridges between the scientific community and the faith community toward "win-win" solutions.

In the midst of this conflict is a patient base that is skeptical of all of the resources. Some assert that each has an inherent conflict of interest in what each claim they are trying to do.

While speaking to a participant in our program he stated to me *"If we all get better… you stop making money…so it's all just a game."* Whereas I understood the premise, I stated it was flawed in that statistics showed and I was confident that addiction, like poverty, would probably remain a constant.

However, the success we experienced in helping them offered hope for those that sought help. Eradicating addiction may not be something that I witness in my life time. Conversely, the powerful impact of hope fueled by the testimonies of former addicts will continue to make much progress in our quest to help as many as desire to be free from addiction.

Therefore I continue to seek best solutions without demonizing a particular premise on the delivery of services. As a man of faith, I believe that God's unprecedented sacrifice of His only begotten Son was motivated by love. Furthermore, I can also believe that a synergistic model that embraces the potential for the extraordinary, and even the supernatural, would best serve a people bound by shame, despair and compulsion.

FAITH-BASED VS. SECULAR RECOVERY MODELS

Rather than endorsing a particular model of treatment or recovery program we sought to address what is most important or frightening to addicted populations. To outline this properly I will use a quote from Kevin P. McClone who wrote in his paper on Psychospirituality of Addiction [19]*"The deeper reality may be that it is more frightening to imagine what it would be like without their addiction of choice. For those struggling with compulsions and addictions, fear and anxiety are intolerable realities that must be avoided rather than the normal realities of living in a world of loss, change and ambiguity. The alcohol, drug, work, food, gambling, addictive relationship, or internet addiction all tend to numb our awareness of these anxieties and tensions."* That fear and anxiety is something that I experienced

---

[19] Psychospirituality of Addiction Pg. 25; Kevin P. Mclone M. Div, Psy.D. published in Seminary Journal, *Volume 9, Winter 2003*

first-hand and witnessed over the course of my studies and vocation for more than 20 years.

Psycho spiritual recovery from addiction involves a fundamental recognition that at the heart of the addictive process is a lost soul traveling down a path seeking peace and an absence from life's pain. Nevertheless, the lost soul is destined for greater alienation from self, others, and God.

At the root of the compulsive and addictive pattern is an identity that feels incomplete, insecure, and lacking adequate resources to cope with life's many changes, losses, and challenges. The impaired reasoning of the addicted usually leads to choosing ineffective coping mechanisms that leave a perpetual void. If left unchecked, the pursuit to fill that void can indulge life-threatening habits.

We found that our faith-based strategy was not conflicting with other recovery models addressing compulsive behavior. Additionally, we found no basis to exclude any other studies as appropriate variants toward building effective strategies of sustaining sobriety. We found new data and studies shared by the Center for Substance Abuse and Treatment as well as others in the mental health community invaluable. Their studies offered more clarity about how the mind and body responded to the chemical make-up of the drugs being abused.

Additionally, we found it essential to build our competencies targeting the behavioral aspects of alcoholism and drug dependence if we were to develop meaningful collaborations within the mental health community. We also embraced the wisdom and guidance offered through Scripture that give credence to another dimension of our existence and struggle. Albert Einstein stated: *"The significant problems we face cannot be solved at the same level of thinking we were at when we created them."*

Elevated or critical thinking has governed much of the reasoning that framed our program model. My goal in writing this book is to point an illuminating light toward the redemptive relationships that set me and others free from compulsive behaviors and have sustained our lives of sobriety.

Henry David Thoreau wrote *"There are a thousand hacking at the branches of evil to one who is striking at the root."* The root causes of evil are probably quite similar to the root causes regarding addiction and substance abuse. With a new emphasis on critical thinking within academia there are "fact-based" premises falling one after another as more data is discovered and tested. It is crucial that we use our critical thinking to consider all of the relevant data available to us and question "best practices" as students that are teachable rather than inflexible tyrants of credible standards.

Our Preserved for Greatness project used innovation to organize the dedication and collective intellect of many service providers to target the volatile needs of our membership.

One of the many lessons learned during this project was that many are unaware of the magnitude and cost of addiction. In addition to the testimonies of lives dramatically changed are the harsh realities that this disease is costing our nation a great deal of money. [20]The National Institute on Drug Abuse presented a study that assessed national costs of substance abuse at more than $484 billion per year. On the other hand, these estimates woefully underestimate the value and impact on relatives and friends that throw in the towel on people struggling with addictions. Too often these invaluable relationships are never restored even after years of sobriety.

Chemical dependencies leading to addiction are associated with patterns having biological, psychological, sociological, and behavioral indicators that confirm someone is *unable* to control their lives or use of the drug.

When we consider the lives that have been altered or lost due to auto accidents associated with DUI the cost increases even more.

We cannot use legislation to eradicate the cost and impact of addiction. Preserved for Greatness was more of an intervention than a preventative model.

20

http://archives.drugabuse.gov/about/welcome/aboutdrugabuse/magnitude/

Additionally, no matter how great the monetary cost, we cannot ignore the importance of programs that are dedicated to providing the resources required to break the chains of addiction.

Also extremely damaging and costly is sexual addiction. This addiction is gaining a lot more popularity largely due to the Internet. However; it is often difficult to measure its degree of compulsion. It is usually under-reported and rarely acted upon unless severe evidence of a high-jacked life that forfeits their resources, reputation, career and esteem of those that love the addicted party. Prominent celebrities have been giving voice to the validity of this disorder through their own very public failures. Somehow the public believes that if someone that has great wealth, great fame, and great access to almost everything they could ever want would confess that this was a problem; then it must be valid.

The stigma of addiction has been largely attributed to people that were perceived as incompetent to handle success, or losers that somehow would never amount to much. In light of the affluent and famous superstars that have recently admitted their struggles with compulsive behaviors, that view is changing.

Pornography and gambling have also gained considerable momentum with the development of Internet sites targeting an insatiable appetite that is allowed to consume as much as a credit card can pay.

[21]"25 million Americans visit cyber-sex sites between 1-10 hours per week; another 4.7 million in excess of 11 hours per week."

Both Gambling and Sex industries have adopted 12 step programs to address the compulsive users within their perspective industries. [22]"Internet gambling has nearly doubled every year since 1997 – in 2001 it exceeded $2 billion. Gambling profits in casinos are more than $30 billion while lotteries are about 17 billion annually."

What is tragically difficult to quantify with numbers or dollars is the damage to the structure of families and the core values of our communities and schools associated with addiction. The number of parents that have been lost to prison terms directly correlates to the number of illegitimate youth. A large number of the youth dropping out of our schools have parents that are incarcerated due to drug related charges. A very high percentage of parents that are incarcerated have children that are on track to engage in criminal behavior leading to prison or death. There are attempts to offset this trend of generational patterns of imprisonment. However, establishing root causes for these patterns and the resources needed to eradicate them has been difficult.

---

[21] (MSNBC/ Stanford/Duquesne Study, Washington Times, 1/26/2000)
[22] http://www.overcominggambling.com/facts.html#Statistics

National and State-wide programs such as TASC have advocated for alternative sentencing strategies to address the disproportionate number of people that are being imprisoned as a result of some involvement with drugs or alcohol. An enhanced form of probation, TASC (Treatment Alternatives for Safe Communities) coordinates its help with the Illinois Dept. of Health and Human Services/ Dept. of Alcohol and Substance Abuse to provide substance abuse assessments and other specified services to the Illinois courts. Our lead organization, R.A.T.E.S Foundation, a National Heritage Foundation worked in coordination with TASC as well to engage with much of the membership we served.

COLLEGE COMES TO P4G

A friend and colleague, Jerry Pizzino visited our facility and fell in love with the members of Preserved for Greatness. Jerry was originally retained to evaluate the program goals and deliverables. However, after completing his evaluation report, he volunteered to contribute college-level leadership classes. Jerry had consulted for a number of universities and large businesses as well. His insights were welcomed and his timely classes contributed invaluable lessons for the membership and staff.

The membership was also instrumental in teaching Jerry life changing principles. He thanked us and them for the time he was allowed to share with them and vowed to do all he could to help raise the awareness for programs like ours.

Friend and colleague, Maureen (Midge) Lansat, LMHC/ Founder/President of Healing and Creative Arts Center also came to our facility and volunteered to help us develop communication competencies. As a State Licensed Supervisor and Trainer of Counselors in Florida, Midge introduced techniques of mirroring, validating and empathizing, helping everyone communicate more effectively.

These were just a couple of the noteworthy contributions afforded to the membership and staff of the "Preserved for Greatness" ATR project.

A DREAM TEAM OF PROFESSIONALS

Indispensable to the principles that were pivotal in guiding our behavior and treatment of our members, was without a doubt, the people. The people I am referring to were not just the staff. Sometimes it was the mother that refused to put a member out of their home. Other times it was a stranger that recognized the hardship and gave some monetary assistance without passing judgment. Often it was a church that stayed open a little later to make sure they could get something to eat from their pantry. Also, we cannot ignore the employer that saw what was happening but gave them one more chance. Most important were often the spouses, children and siblings that gathered in prayer and support in hopes of a full recovery. At times it took a combination of people that were not directly connected to our program that helped to facilitate the help needed. On more days than I could record in any book, God worked with and through people of different cultures, races, genders, and ages to touch the lives of everyone connected with *"Preserved For Greatness."*

We applied the lyrics stated in Hezekiah Walker's song: *"You are important to me, I need you to survive"* to our program and our lives. Everyone was important and we expressed that point intentionally.

With that in mind, it is very important that I acknowledge that we were blessed to have an incredibly gifted staff of people that sacrificed and shared far more than was outlined in this brief expose of Preserved for Greatness. Over the years, this program served more than 2,500 members and it required a great deal of contribution from professionals locally and nationally.

We could not have managed the fiscal reporting required for this program without the National Heritage Foundation. Their humble and modest staffs were always seeking ways to be flexible and help us to sustain through our challenges.

We had a very special relationship with A Safe Haven and will forever be indebted to their professionalism and willingness to work with us, allowing for the innovation that we tried to implement in this pioneering project.

There were staff members that received little or no recognition in this book whose efforts are forever written on the hearts of me and the membership. Your tireless efforts will never be forgotten and I pray your rewards are stored in heaven for you.

To frame the thousands of memories from this project was impossible for me. This was a modest attempt in sharing some of the extraordinary stories birthed out of this project. However, there was certainly enough material to write a great mini-series if that was my task. Regrettably, this book is all that I can present at this time.

Please consider this attempt as Volume 1 in a series of Volumes that are soon to come. For those that are discontented by the lack of references to your contribution, I would encourage you to compose your own creations to capture your contributions more precisely.

ATR was one of several programs being considered for budgeting. A government paid evaluator came from D.C. to view our program. She wanted to see evidence of the program's viability and effectiveness. We recorded a sample of an unrehearsed meeting where she was able to hear testimonials from the members who attended the program. Here are a few abbreviated statements from that meeting:

Dressed very sharply, a tall Black man stood and addressed the evaluator saying: "*I done lived my life. Now I'm trying to be born again. I'm trying to live the other life. They say you get two. My other life is gone. I've put those childish things away and now I'm trying to become a man.*"

Another young woman stood up and said "*In this place I have learned to have humility... that love is patient and it is kind. I learned that here. I gained my respect from my children. I gained my respect from my mother. I'm learning how to love my mother 'cause I didn't know how to love my mother. My mother was addicted also. Now I know how to help other people. I have a husband who is struggling with addiction. Pastor Jamal taught me how to love my husband, not be his mother... We have to learn how to love other people that are hurting. I learned how to apply the Scriptures to my life and live them. I take one day at a time. As a matter of fact, I take one minute at a time.*"

Another young woman boldly declared: *"I've been raped in the streets. I've robbed people in the streets. I stole from my family. I stole from my kids. But today my kids love me today. My family loves me. Today my family go out and leave the door open and give me keys to the doors. I never had keys to nobody's door."*

In a separate testimony and interview, a young man with a sorted history of bi-polar disorders and addiction stated this: *"What's happened to me has been a miracle through working with these people... and a miracle for my mother and my kids, cause I was no good for my kids and was not a son to my parents... They say you need a psychic change in Alcoholic Anonymous... drugs controlled my mind. I could never be straight unless I got locked up or an ambulance came to get me from a street corner somewhere...Once a drug addict always a drug addict, I realize that's not true cause I've seen people that have been through the same things I been through that have been clean for a year or 2-3 years and that let me know that I could do it."*

These testimonies and others provided from around the country proved the validity of our program and fortunately the funding for ATR continued. Unfortunately, revisions to the program prevented us from being able to continue the "Preserved for Greatness" model. There were many more testimonies I could share because most of these members were so pleased to be a part of any sustaining effort for this program. We are all very grateful to have been given the opportunity to develop greatness in others.

IN CONCLUSION

In this unprecedented effort towards recovery, we were fortunate to have celebrated new jobs, weddings, children born, birthdays of members and staff, anniversaries of sobriety and even mourned deaths!

These high spirited emotional benchmarks represented new social norms that restored hope and encouraged members that they were building competencies in self-control. Many began to believe they could press through threatening urges to re-engage in the temptations of their youth. Most continued to come to the program long after funding resources were exhausted and even after employment opportunities were initiated.

I am still receiving updates of those which we officiated marriage ceremonies, and I am extremely pleased to report that all are still married and sober!

[23]*"Greater love has no one than this, than to lay down one's life for his friends."*

I applaud all of those dedicated toward helping recovering people to gain their independence to renew an interdependence that redeems their self-respect. Difficult times come for us all. We overcome those times best while we are helping others to be restored to the greatness they were predestined to share.

---

[23] John 15:13 NKJV

ACKNOWLEDGEMENTS

I am forever mindful of the contributions of people in my life that have helped me to stay the course of this journey I am traveling. This book is the fruit of many who deposited love, support, knowledge, faith, and encouragement into me. Ranked among the most influential is my very beautiful, gifted and faithful wife, Dr. Margaret Jamal. I am humbled by the volume of stamina and genius that God has gifted her with. This work would have been just another "incomplete" on my list of well intentioned ventures if not for her steady guidance and support.

This book frames a "once in a lifetime" experience with people that have forever been knitted in my heart as family and friends. Some people go through an entire life without experiencing the mutually gratifying dynamics embedded in social services. The late Rev. Hazel Fort framed that burning desire to engage and to help others where you can within my heart. I can't imagine what my life would be like without the model of love and selflessness she provided for me. I truly hope that she is pleased with this work she inspired in me and the others she touched.

Additionally, my children have not been acknowledged within this book, however, I have relied upon their sacrifice and faithfulness in order to pursue these dreams to help others. I have fallen short of the mark as the father each so richly deserved on more than one occasion. There were far too many nights and days that

I gave to others during a time when they needed me, and for their sacrifice I will forever be in their debt. Many do not know how difficult it is to be thrown in the pathway of dangerous and sometimes treacherous people. I failed to insulate my children from everything that was toxic and they endured to love me still. Thank you, Aisha, Gina, Asia, Joshua, and Elijah. You are forever my gifts from heaven that I will always cherish and love.

To my siblings, alive and those transitioned, I will forever try to honor your efforts to guide and protect me from things I didn't understand.

To the professionals that I worked with on this project, I continue to salute your dedication and sacrifice as well. My hope is that you also viewed this experience with Preserved for Greatness and ATR as extraordinary and life changing.

To Dr. Theodora Binyon-Taylor, I will never forget the patience, guidance and faith that you afforded our collaborative, our membership and me specifically. To Dr. Tommy Williams, thank you for the education and credentials. To Judge John P. Kirby, my sincere thanks and appreciation for your support and advocacy.

To Pastor Keith Brady, Apostle C.D. Bush, Rev. Dr. Margaret Jamal, Mrs. Candra Chavda, Malcom Burgess, Pastor David Turnipseed, Mrs. Carolyn Bush, Pastor Richard Redmond, Stanley Martin and all of the staff at National Heritage Foundation, I can never truly appropriate the level of respect and admiration I have for the privilege granted to work with you.

To Allen (Skip) Land of A Safe Haven, I will always remember that in the midst of an anti-faith-based climate, you were willing to befriend and partner with our collaborative. We could not have grown as we did without your respect and willingness to work with us.

Finally, to all of the Peer Coaches and membership that lent me and our staff your trust and perseverance, I will forever consider our time together as priceless. I am sure that you can understand the necessity to mask identities in order keep the confidence and discretion of everyone that made up these wonderful stories. I will continue to pray for each of you. I hope that each of you will be honored by the references within this book. You taught me so much more than I have been able to frame within these pages.

Please join me in thanking God Almighty for choosing a wretch like me to save and participate in His plan to reveal those that He has "Preserved for Greatness."

Rev. Aaron Jamal PhD